PRESS TO POSSESS THE PROMISE

DISCOVER THE PRINCIPLES TO HELP ACTIVATE GOD'S PROMISES IN YOUR LIFE

By

Elder Karen J. Fowler

Press to Possess the Promise
By Elder Karen J Fowler

Copyright 2021

All rights reserved. No part of this book may be reproduced or transmitted in any form or by any means whatsoever without express written permission from the author, except in the case of brief quotations embodied in critical articles and reviews. Please refer all pertinent questions to the publisher.

All scriptures are taken from the King James Version or the New American Standard Bibles unless otherwise denoted.

ISBN: 978-1-7364096-0-2

Dedications

I absolutely cannot express how grateful I am to my husband, Mark. His love and support encouraged me to "keep pressing". We are still an effective team!

To my Mother (Sweet) for your love, affection, and every prayer that you have prayed I am eternally grateful.

To my Dad, thank you for the blessing that you spoke over my life and all of the pep talks that gave me the confidence I needed to step out on faith.

To Antoinette & Jaye you have my heart, always!

Finally, to my friend forever, Rhonda Marie Guy, I'll see you in His Glory!

Table of Contents

Dedications iii

Chapter 1: The Prophecies 1

Chapter 2: The Purpose 13

Chapter 3: The Principles 25

Chapter 4: The Pattern 53

Chapter 5: The Precepts 65

Chapter 6: The Process 75

Chapter 7: The Participation 97

Chapter 8: The Patience 103

Chapter 9: The Partners 111

Chapter 10: The Press 119

Chapter 11: The Ultimate Promise 131

Afterword 134

End Notes 135

Chapter 1
THE PROPHECIES

What had happened was...

I will never forget the big white Bible storybook. It was a gift for my birthday from two of my mother's friends, a Caucasian couple whose names I do not remember. I was 5 or 6 years old then, at most, because my baby sister had not yet been born. I cherished that big book so much that I wrapped the cover in some plastics that my parent's clothes had come in from the dry cleaner.

Recently, while at my mother's home, I recounted the book and asked her who that couple was. They would often visit and sit on her bed, and they would chat for, what seemed to be, hours. I always thought they worked with her. Or perhaps, they were in the music business, like my parents. Oddly enough, my mother remembered the book but said no such couple ever came to our home. That was unbelievable! But it was even weirder that she could not remember who gave me the big white Bible storybook. My eyes wailed with tears. Suddenly, at that moment, I realized the ALMIGHTY GOD had chosen me from childhood. I knew, in that instance, that He sent His angels to direct my path.

Prophetic Encounter One~

It was a Sunday evening worship service in 2002. During the sermon, the atmosphere shifted, and my pastor became a ball of fire. He laid hands on the infirmed and imparted so much.

In those days, I was the producer of our telecast. While in the media room capturing this awesome move, a fellow staff rushed in and told me that the pastor was calling all staff. I almost discounted what he was telling me because neither the technical director nor I heard my pastor make such a request over the monitors. This was unusual because, in the Edit Suite, we could see and hear everything in the sanctuary. However, the young man assured me that the request was real, and I needed to hurry! Immediately, I went into the sanctuary, where the staff lined up for an impartation. Amazingly, I was the last person in the queue. In retrospect, it was significant to me, and I was anticipating what would happen next.

The atmosphere was supercharged. Literally, I felt the glory of God in the room. Saints were crying; some lay prostrate on the sanctuary floor; others stood in reverence and awe at the move of God. It was electrifying! As I approached my pastor, his eyes were like fire! He had been ministering so fervently. When he looked at me, it was as if he was looking directly into my spirit. My pastor, who is a Bishop, took off his suit coat, which I had never seen him do before. Then placed the coat on my shoulders, affirmed my calling to preach the Gospel of the Kingdom, and took me by the hand, leading me to the seat positioned on the right of his chair and made me sit on it. He turned to speak into the lives of the congregation, and as I sat there in total awe, another pastor squatted next to me and asked, "Do you see where he sat you?" I didn't notice it, but I was seated in the chair where many anointed preachers had sat. Tommy Tenney, Bishop Jackie McCullough, and Bishop Iona Locke, just a few generals of faith who had graced our church, and literally, I sat where they sat. I began to weep. The Bishop turned to me again and said, "The LORD said that you will preach to thousands! Then, as if being corrected in the Spirit, he said, "NO! MILLIONS!"

Prophetic Encounter 2~

A year or more later, I was invited to be the guest soloist at a pastor's revival. Following Holy Spirit's leading, I was led to sing a song that I knew the music minister did not know. I whispered to him, "Please, just flow with me. Just catch me in the spirit". I sensed that I would be operating as a psalmist that night. As I began to worship, the Wind of God began to blow, and it was the most beautiful experience I had ever had! The spiritual setting was conducive for the prophetic.

That night, Prophetess Sandy Archangel, from New Iberville, Louisiana, was the Guest Revivalist. She stood from her seat on the chancel, approached the pulpit and immediately, began to pray. Her prayer transitioned into prophetic utterance. With her eyes still closed, she said, "And for the blessed one who led us in the worship tonight, the Father has placed you high upon a pedestal and covered you up. But He is going to uncover you that the world may see how we are to worship Him." From that night onward, I pondered God's promise in my heart.

Prophetic Encounter 3~

"She is MY International Evangelist!" These were the awe-inspiring words that sent me into a tailspin after "a once-in-a-lifetime" 5:00 AM prayer service in 2004. A woman whom I had never seen before spoke this powerful prophetic word to me. I can safely say she had never seen me before either. She was not a member of our local assembly. To this day, I cannot remember her face, and I do not know her name. However, her words were extremely powerful and even more frightening to me.

After the prayer service, she beckoned for my attention as I sat with a group of ladies. At first, I thought she was speaking to someone else; but she specifically pointed at me out of about 10 people. Initially, I thought she wanted information about the church. As I stood and began to walk towards her, I realized that she was moving me away from the group. So, I began to think it is a crucial, personal discussion, and I walked with her towards the center of the sanctuary. She began to tell me that as I entered the sanctuary that morning, the LORD spoke to her clearly, "She is MY International Evangelist!"

As I was processing her words, I could not help but rehearse, in my heart, conversations that I had been having with the LORD. At that time in my life, I was going through a wilderness experience and in a very dark place. I was at an all-time spiritually low level because I had just, within days, been passed over for ordination. It was a struggle to be faithful to the ministry, where I had not only served and sacrificed so much but also where I worked as an employee. Yet, the ultimate struggle was the fierce fight against my own flesh to become bitter.

As this nameless woman moved in the Gift of Knowledge, I felt the Wind of God once again; but this time I went to the floor. As I lay there in a fetal position, she laid hands on my feet and prayed for me. Then, she was gone. She left me there on the floor. In fact, all the people who remained after the prayer service were leaving. I heard one of the leaders say, "We're going to Shoney's." I heard another person ask, "Where is Karen?" Someone else responded, "She's still on the floor."

That morning after the amazing prayer service, I repented of my attitude and disposition. I asked the Father to forgive me for disregarding and disrespecting the previous prophecies because my life was seemingly going backward instead of forward. Then, the heavens opened for me. The LORD revealed to me that my sins had been forgiven. He had called me before I was born. He blessed me by letting me know that degrees and certificates are man's standard of measurement. I had been Chosen!

Each of these prognostications, spoken by the Spirit of the LORD over my life, was intertwined with the other and had to do with international ministry.

At 11:10~

On December 29, 2007, I had an awesome prophetic dream. In the dream, I, along with some others, was at the residence of two prominent spiritual leaders; a male and female pastor. Their home was positioned on a hill in a neighborhood. These pastors stepped out of the house and moved towards their Mercedes Benz. One was a black car while the other was champagne. They were both casually dressed.

When they got into their vehicles, his car, the black, was parked directly behind hers, which was in front of their garage. There were other people, along with me, standing at the opened garage door. Strangely, she took off ahead of him like a bat out of hell, driving recklessly, and he was making every attempt to catch up with her. As I stood in the garage watching them, they drove off to my left. When they were out of my view, I could hear the tires shrieking. The recklessness of her driving caused an accident. We all heard the crash, but we could not see the accident.

Somehow the pastor had gotten behind a slow traveling vehicle. He was very agitated that he could not get to her. He rushed out of his car and ran to where the accident occurred. One of the people in the garage with me said, "We need to go down and pray."

I told another person, "You should call the insurance company because you know about their policies." He responded, "I'm not doing that." About that time, two people escorted, her on foot, back to the house. She was banged up and a little bloody but walking. She would survive. However, the pastor and some of the members of their ministry, who had gone to the scene, began to pray. I could see and hear them in the spirit, praying as I stood at the foot of the garage. They were positioned in a field between me and where the crash had actually occurred. He was leading a fiery, fervent prayer saying, "Thank you Jesus, for the money! Thank you Jesus for the money!" He repeated this several times. This was anticipatory because of the accident his wife had been in, which she had caused. But he continued the chant.

These scenes were so disturbing that I exclaimed, "I've got to get out of here! I've got to get out of here!" I noticed that as I said this, I was already out of the garage and was in the street. I turned to my left to go to my car, and immediately, the day turned into night. At that point, I realized I was wearing my navy-blue trench coat. Suddenly, from behind me to my left, two huge longhorn bulls, one black and one red came charging my way. They began to run around me. Oddly, I was not afraid of them. I did the old cowboy yell, "Ya, Ya!" as they circled me. They came back around, but this time, after passing me, they settled in a driveway in front of a house across the street. They stood there, almost tamed-like, side-by-side. Then I noticed a beautiful black and white collie appeared in front of them, sitting obediently in front of the bulls.

As I started walking to my car, the collie hopped up on the hood, and I sat there playing with the dog until I realized I needed to go. In fact, I said again, "I've got to get out of here." I got in my car and decided to call my hairstylist, whose name is Destiney. I dialed her number, and my dear friend, a true intercessor, answered Destiney's phone. As we began to talk I heard Destiney ask to whom she was speaking. After telling her who was on the phone, I said, "Ask Destiney if I can come and get my hair done?" I heard Destiney say, "Tell Karen I said come on." With that, I turned on my car engine to drive to her place. I made a right turn and then left turn to stop at a stop sign where I was confronted with the biggest digital clock I had ever seen. It reads '11:10' in gigantic red numbers. I thought, "Oh my goodness, it's late." I made a right turn again, headed to Destiney, and the dream ended.

<u>Fast Forward~</u>

For several years, the Holy Spirit began to unravel the meaning of that night vision. For several years, the prophetic dream was always before me. I started working for a human services agency in 2007. In 2012, we relocated our offices into another building. I worked in that building for at least two years before I saw it. I passed it every single day, except on weekends, of course. How could I have not been paying attention?

Outside the office building was a clock. It was a four-sided clock with beautiful brass details that looked like an antique. There were four lion heads holding rings in their mouths. I knew that the clock did not work! But one day, I looked up at it as I had undoubtedly done many times and the floodgates opened as I finally saw it! Low and behold, the time had stopped on the Roman numerals, 11:10. Ah! Remember the dream. It had always been at that particular time!

After about a year, I was so excited to drive by the clock and saw it working. The *Chronos* was now prophesying, and I knew that I was getting closer to my *Kairos* moment.

There was such a press in my spirit. I was wrestling with a major decision. I sensed that the LORD was calling me away from the local assembly, where I had worshipped and served for almost 20 years. To leave, I would be giving up a much-needed supplemental income and departing from people I intensely cared about. After much prayer, fasting, and spiritual counsel, it was final! The LORD had spoken, and I would not interfere! Time was up! The exit strategy given by the LORD was not to bring in 2016 with the ministry. On December 31, 2015, at the prophetic time of 11:10 pm, I was to submit my letter of resignation from all ministerial and administrative duties at the ministry via e-mail. As I sat in my living room during early Morning Prayer, I asked the LORD why 11:10 pm? The Spirit of God sat beside me and said, "The children of Israel left Egypt at night. It is the LORD's will that you do the same." At that moment, I wept as I settled the matter in my heart.

At the Annual Watch Night Celebration, at approximately 10:00 pm, December 31, 2015, I led praise and worship before that congregation for the last time. My resignation Email was sent at the prophetic hour, which was 11:10 pm, and I exited the premises. It was a very cold night, but I felt the warmth and peace of God that truly surpassed my understanding.

These are the initial experiences that have led me on this amazing journey that I now travel. What has God spoken concerning you? What experiences have you had that you can now trace back to God? I know a believer who told me that as a child, at playtime with her siblings, they would make believe they were students in a classroom and she insisted on being the teacher. After graduating from college, she became a sales representative for a Fortune 500 company. She never considered teaching as an adult until the dean of the school at her church asked her if she would be interested in teaching a class. She told me it never dawned on her that GOD was preparing her, as a child, to teach. She is now teaching, not in a traditional classroom, but in the Body of the Messiah.

As for me, I can go back to many encounters and instances from childhood, where the LORD's hand was evident. However, the most invaluable experience was the day it was revealed in my mother's house. It was never so potent and pertinent, the way in which the Spirit of the LORD opened my mother and my eyes to how God had practically been working in my entire life. That big white Bible Storybook was my true sign that I was called to be one of the guardians of the Father's story.

II Corinthians 13:1 says, *"In the mouth of two or three witnesses shall every word be established."* From my testimony, I have had three prophecies spoken to me from three different channels coupled with other personal prophetic dreams. Undoubtedly, ELOHIYM's Word is confirmed and genuine. Also, reading this ACTUAL book is proof of YAHUAH's promise coming to pass in my life.

Chapter 2
THE PURPOSE

As iron sharpens iron…
Proverbs 27:17a

For the sake of clarity, let me say at the onset that this book is intended for the person who knows their existential essence. It is not about finding your purpose or discovering your destiny. There are hundreds of other books that can minister to that particular need in your life. However, to get the full benefit of this work, you should be able to say what Yahusha said when He was interrogated by Pilate, "To this end was I born, and for this cause came I into the world, that I should bear witness unto the truth," (John 18:37).

To help us in this journey, let us define, from a Biblical standpoint, the word *purpose*? In Paul's letter to the church at Ephesus, in Ephesians 1:9-11, he explains how God accomplishes His desire and plan of bringing all things in heaven and earth together in the Messiah. In Yahusha, all things will conform to the preordained will of the Divine. The entire economy of God is interconnected with what He has set forth in the heavens. Hence, no believer is an accident. No believer in the Messiah is a happenstance, random phenomenon; but rather, a part of the divine design from the beginning of time, according to Romans 8:28, *"And we know that God causes all things to work together for good to those who love God, to those who are called according to His purpose."* Here, it is necessary to point out two key terms. The first is the word "called." In Greek, it means being called with a personal objective. A more descriptive word for this term is "invited" or "welcomed." This reveals that we have been divinely appointed and selected to participate in His divine orchestration.

The other key term is "purpose," which means setting forth or setting up something in its place, but in plain view. The inference is that ELOHIYM has placed all things, especially future events and happenings, before His Mind to see them distinctly. They are entirely exposed to Him. With these two terms, we know that we have been invited and appointed by the Infinite One to participate in His predetermined and divinely designed work in Yahusha Ha'Mashiach. Indeed, YHWH has unique plans and purposes for each believer. However, we must understand that His purpose is directed towards the advancement of His Kingdom and not according to human agenda.

If you have not discovered your purpose "to this end," I suggest you pray fervently to discover your reason for being. The Father might have purposed you to be a children's teacher in Sunday school, and consequently, you will influence children who would become battle-axes for the Kingdom. Whatever your purpose might be, it is important you do it heartily and according to the desire of the Father.

To those who do not have a burning desire to do what has been revealed because of preconceived ideas, I challenge you to read this book. It will enlighten you on the severity of using what has been installed within you to meet a greater need than your own.

This book is for the individual who has, at least, an inkling of what the ALMIGHTY GOD has planned for his life. It has been written to encourage people who are yet to step into their actual calling. More specifically, it is a long letter from a dear comrade endeavoring to sharpen your countenance. Many of you have been discouraged because you have had the awesome privilege of seeing an excerpt of yourself doing what you have been called to do. You may have seen it in a dream, vision, or it was a prophecy, and your spirit bore witness to it, and now you hold fast to the promise.

It could be that the Father has put an insatiable desire within you to do a specific task. You may not entirely understand it, yet you cannot rid yourself off this aspiration. It is an intense feeling, and you long for its manifestation. You have waited for months and even years for your "breakthrough." You have found yourself doubting if it would ever come to pass. Was it just a dream? Was it a figment of your imagination? With many of you, the Father has spoken specifically to you, and now you ponder on whether you heard Him correctly. Is that desire really something He will establish in your life? Psalm 37:4 states, *"He will give you the desire of your heart."* My friend, I want to encourage you not to faint. If our Father has given you a promise, it shall be established.

As I have clarified to whom this book has been written, I must also express that this discourse is not just about obtaining the material things (houses, cars, or money) that you may bask in your own grandeur. If your promise is only for you, then it is a selfish desire to be outside and away from the Will of God. When the Father distributes gifts, they are not to be hoarded or used according to self-benefit only, but for the benefit of His Kingdom. However, my words are not designed to appease your appetite to acquire material things; I simply want you to understand the main focus. Yahusha cautions us, in Luke 12:15, about having a covetous or greedy spirit, *"A man's life does not consist in the abundance of things which he possesses."* Another translation says, *"Not even when one has abundance does his life consist of possessions."* In YAHUAH's Economy, acquiring wealth is irrelevant if it does not effectuate His Kingdom. Materialistic possessions do not define who you are. Am I a basher of prosperity? Not on your life. But as a comrade, I caution you as Yahusha did to beware of every form of greed.

I am of the persuasion that wealth is not the ultimate focus of Father's divine purpose for you. **His plan has a greater degree of reason than mere personal materialistic gain.** It has been prophetically announced to some of you that wealth would be in your hands, and GOD be praised for it. However, I do not believe that the great riches will be for you to build big barns for yourself, but rather for the promotion of Kingdom work in many capacities. Interestingly, when God sees our desire to multiply Kingdom expectations, He simply blesses us with 'all things' (Matthew 6:33).

Yahusha further warned with His parable in Luke 12:21. It is about a rich fool who stored up treasures for himself. As a believer, if we store up treasure for ourselves, it is likely that we will not be rich toward God. Being rich is not condemnation. There are many rich icons in scripture, and their possessions were of great assistance in the programs of YHWH. The excessive love of money has become the root of all evil desires, and it has taken many away from the Father. Paul echoes this truth to Timothy, testifying how some sought-after and longed for it, and wandered from the faith, and pierced themselves through with many sorrows (1 Timothy 6:10).

Again, the intention of this book is to excite and inspire you concerning your promise. It is a guide to ensure that ELOHIYM's promise comes to pass in your life. My earnest desire is that you will be encouraged to press through all uncertainty, pain, doubt, and disbelief. Henceforth, no more excuses. PRESS TO POSSESS GOD'S PROMISE!

This is not a manual to teach you how to receive the promise of YAHUAH. The promise has already been given. There are, however, preliminaries in scripture that I have discovered. These fundamentals should be actualized if we are to participate in the plan of GOD and bring glory to His High Name. There are some imperative steps that each of us must take in order to see the promise manifested in our life.

Here I would like to emphasize a crucial element, a critical key that must not be overlooked nor taken for granted. It is the simple but profound truth that the Father is not subjected to anything or anyone. He is sovereign and completely independent of systems and protocols. All power and glory belong to Him. He does not necessitate legalisms and religiosities to accomplish His mission. Nor does He demand that all of His Kingdom citizens have a doctorial degree before they can be direct representatives. However, educational degrees could be necessary in order to effectuate the Kingdom in the halls of higher learning, politics, or economics. Conversely, not all are called to stringent collegiate studies. If this is your obligation, I charge you to keep at it until you obtain those degrees, as they will indeed glorify your Father, which is in heaven.

The ALMIGHTY GOD needs neither validation nor approval; He is Absolute. His power is supreme. In scripture, we witness Him working through a variety of personalities and professions. Some individuals were educated while others were not. When He worked through the lives of His initial Apostles, the rulers and elders knew that these disciples were uneducated and untrained in the orthodoxies of the Torah. Yet, they could not deny that these men knew the veracity of YAHUAH's sacred Word. Alternatively, Apostle Paul was a Hellenistic Jew. This indicates that he spoke and wrote Greek.[1] This afforded him the advantage when addressing the Greek-speaking echelon concerning the gospel of the Messiah. However, in either case, educated or not, it must be noted that it is the empowerment of the Holy Spirit that truly makes the difference.

Concerning you, it may be of interest that the LORD did not convene a counsel or consult a committee to determine your qualifications for Kingdom work. Nor did He check our resume` to conclude if we had the necessary credentials or acceptable pedigree before He appointed us. He did not request, neither did He require our references. There was no competition for an opportunity from Him to make you a promise. In His infinite wisdom, He determined that you, with all of your predilections, would be fit for the promise. The Father had no discussions with anyone about anything concerning your mission… including you!

Apostle Paul teaches in his letter to the church at Corinth that we do not belong to ourselves. YAH has purchased us with the Blood of the Lamb. In Psalm 95:7, we find that *"He is our God; and we are the people of His pasture, and the sheep of His hand."* He

---

[1] Bruce, F.F. (1999). *PAUL Apostle of the Heart Set Free*. (William B. Eerdmans Publishing Company)

entrusted you, His possession, with His possessions. The gift, talent, and ability that the Father has given you are His! The promise that He has made to do a work through you is His Promise, for His purpose!

Contrary to what we have been taught, GOD does not ALWAYS confirm the thing He will do in and through us prior manifestation. This revelation can be found in 1 Samuel 16. This chapter provides an account of YAHUAH sending the Prophet Samuel to Jesse, the Bethlehemite's house. Jesse is significant because his lineage goes back to Rahab, an Amorite, who lived in Jericho. She was associated with the spies that Joshua sent out to survey the Promised Land. After the fall of Jericho, Rahab is referred to as being the wife of Salmon, a prince in the tribe of Judah, who was one of the two spies she sheltered. In turn, she became the mother of Boaz. Boaz married Ruth, the Moabite daughter-in-law of Naomi. To them was born a son Obed, the father of Jesse, the father of David through whose line Yahusha was born. [2]

YAHUAH instructed the Prophet Samuel that he would find King Saul's replacement at Jesse's house. Saul was the first King of Israel after a long

---

[2] https://www.biblegateway.com/resources/all-women-bible/rahab

stretch of being led by Judges. Upon arrival at Jesse's house, Samuel, the Prophet/Judge, conducted a kind of pass-and-review wherein Jesse made seven of his sons pass before him. But YAH had not chosen any of them. David, Jesse's youngest son, was tending his father's sheep in the meadows. I imagine that he was singing love songs to the LORD and writing the lyrics to some of the greatest Psalms, which are still being sung today. While being faithful to his father's sheep-herding business, the LORD was teaching him the grave resemblances between human beings and sheep. It is my belief that David was even being developed the area of prophecy and honing his musical ability, as well as learning to fight fearlessly against foes that were larger than him. He fought lions and bears to protect his father's precious commodity. However, while being about his earthly father's business, he had no idea that his heavenly Father had chosen him to be the next king of the commonwealth of Israel.

In 1 Samuel 16:11 (NASB), Samuel asked Jesse, *"Are these all the children?"* To which Jesse replied, *"There remains yet the youngest... he is tending the sheep."* Then Samuel said to Jesse, *"Send and take him; for we will not sit down until he comes...."* When Samuel saw David, a handsome, healthy-looking young man with beautiful eyes, the LORD said, *"This is he!"* It was the Prophet who said to David, "you are our next king." David could not say, "Well, the LORD did not tell me this, so it cannot be true." Nor did he say, "The LORD told me this; I knew it; this is just a confirmation."

Because YAHUAH is our Creator, He reserves the right to act, as He will with each of us. We have all been born at a particular time in history for a specific purpose. Some, like Queen Esther, have been brought into the world's domain that you might use your negotiating skills and other God-given assets and abilities with governments to benefit the blessed Kingdom of YAH. Others have been washed in the Blood of the Lamb so that you might participate in carrying the Gospel to the nations. This, my beloved, is the ultimate purpose for the promise. It is your duty and responsibility, in whatever capacity the FATHER has called or invited you, to work with Him by *"holding forth the word of life"* (Philippians 2:16). More specifically, your gift is designed so you can exhibit the Word of YAHUAH, which is Yahusha our Messiah, through the life that you now live in Him.

The promise that He has given to you is for the benefit of others so that the Kingdom of YAH may be established on the earth. This is why He has revealed His purpose to you. The Father promised you, and

He is committed and faithful to fulfill His promises in your life so that you may share in the proclamation that Yahusha is LORD! The promise is not for you ALONE! The promise is for the Father and for those that He has prepared it for. This might be just for a person, a small group of people, or billions of people. Regardless, embrace it.

Chapter 3

THE PRINCIPLES

The Beginning –

In the beginning, God
Genesis 1:1

The Word of YHWH is the source of truth. It is the embodiment of knowledge, conduct, procedure, and systems of reasoning. The Bible is used as a basis for not only prediction but also action. There are keys and crucial elements that must be grasped if we are to see the manifestations of God's promise. I believe these principles are necessary and will assist us greatly as we press to possess the promise.

Also, we must regard the laws or decrees of ELOHIYM. In his theological dictionary, Reverend Charles Buck defines decrees as "God's settled purposes, whereby he foreordains whatsoever comes to pass."[3]

For a moment, consider the unalterable principles and laws that are on the earth. From creation, these decrees are yet in effect. A long seam can be traced from the book of Genesis to the Revelation of Yahusha the Messiah. Remarkably, these decrees have never changed. Psalm 119:89 declares, *"Forever, O LORD, Thy word is settled in the heavens."* His word is everlasting, and it stands firmly to accomplish that which He has purposed. For example, the unalterable principle of the four seasons; winter, spring, summer, and fall. This order has never changed. Not once has spring come in fall. Although, in some geographical areas, at times, it can feel like spring in the fall season. However, this does not change the season. It is only the temperature of the season that has changed. From the time the Creator said, "LET THERE BE," things have been *being* ever since. Not once has the sun not come up at dawn. Not once have the terrestrial planets floated out of their solar systems. From the beginning of their creation, the earth and other planets are functioning in

---

[3] Buck, Charles. Entry for 'Decrees of God'. Charles Buck Theological Dictionary. http://www.studylight.org/dictionaries/cbd/d/decrees-of-god.html. 1802.

accordance with the law of nature that ELOHIYM set in motion through His "LET THERE BE." The grass is still growing from underneath the earth. Cows have not evolved into flying creatures. Fishes still need water to live. Man is still breathing oxygen and exhaling carbon dioxide. Things are still in their natural order. Everything is still operating, for all intents and purposes. Just the way He intended from the beginning. Just as these universal laws are non-negotiable, the spiritual principles of YHWH are non-negotiable and should be recognized if we want to lay hold of the promise.

The Principle of Investment

In the gospel, according to Matthew, Yahusha teaches one of several parables about what the Kingdom of YAH is like. This parable is about a businessman who is setting his business affairs in order before going on a long journey.

(Matthew 25:14-29)

"For it is just like a man about to go on a journey, who called his own servants and entrusted his possessions to them." To one he gave five talents, to another, two, and to another, one, each according to his own ability; and he went on his journey."

"Immediately the one who had received the five talents went and traded with them, and gained five more talents." In the same manner the one who had received the two talents gained two more. *"But he who received the one talent went away, and dug a hole in the ground and hid his master's money."*

"Now after a long time the master of those servants came and settled accounts with them." The one who had received the five talents came up and brought five more talents, saying, 'Master, you entrusted five talents to me. See, I have gained five more talents.' *"His master said to him, 'Well done, good and faithful servant. You were faithful with a few things, I will put you in charge of many things; enter into the joy of your master.'"*

"Also the one who had received the two talents came up and said, 'Master, you entrusted two talents to me. See, I have gained two more talents.' His master said to him, 'Well done good and faithful servant. You were faithful with a few things, I will put you in charge of many things; enter into the joy of your master.'"

"And the one also who had received the one talent came up and said, 'Master, I knew you to be a hard man, reaping where you did not sow and gathering

where you scattered no seed. And I was afraid, and went away and hid your talent in the ground. See, you have what is yours.'"

"But his master answered and said to him, 'you wicked, lazy servant, you knew that I reap where I did not sow and gather where I scattered no seed. Then you ought to have put my money in the bank, and on my arrival, I would have received my money back with interest. Therefore take away the talent from him, and give it to the one who has the ten talents.' For to everyone who has, more shall be given, and he will have an abundance;'"

I have a Bachelor of Science Degree in Business Management. One of the key concepts learned in my business finance class was ROI or Return on Investment. In simple terms, it is the benefit that an investor receives from an investment. The stakeholders invest in stocks, real estate, and commodities with the expectation that such investments will yield high or lucrative dividends or sell at a profitable price. This is the sole purpose for participating in the marketplace; to profit.

The parable mentioned above of Yahusha reveals to us this principle or law of investment. We have been given every resource from the Father, our Source. These resources come in many forms, such as time, talents, and abilities. In the Kingdom, the unique thing about investment is that the time, gift, or ability comes from ELOHIYM. He has entrusted us with His resources. As James 1:17 informs us, *"Every good and perfect gift comes from the Father."* The gift or the resource is His. Unlike in the world's system, for instance, wherein an investor purchases stocks or invests in that which someone has else developed, created, or is selling. We are not owners of the gift; we are stewards. Gifts, in God's economy, are benefactions and bounties. Benefactions are donations or investments.[4] Bounties are the good things or generous rewards that are given freely and in large amounts.[5] The contributions of God were given as part of our inheritance in Messiah.

The parable in Matthew's gospel account further confirms that the Father is the true Investor, and He is expecting a RETURN on His investment:

> *"But his master answered and said to him, 'you wicked, lazy servant, you knew that I reap where I did not sow and gather where I scattered no seed. Then you ought to have put my money in the bank, and on my arrival I would have received my money back with interest. Therefore take away the talent from*

---

[4] https://www.dictionary.com/browse/benefaction?s=t

[5] https://www.merriam-webster.com/dictionary/bounty

> *him, and give it to the one who has the ten talents.' For to everyone who has, more shall be given, and he will have an abundance;"*
> *Matthew 25:26-29.*

The businessman in Yahusha's parable entrusted his possessions to his servants while giving each servant a designated amount. Additionally, each servant was given what the businessman felt he had the capacity to handle. Here, we see that there is a divine expectation for each of us. It is our duty to use His possessions to fulfill His promise or complete His mission on the earth. We are responsible for using these resources that multiply or increase in value. Since He gives liberally, He is also expecting a copious return. This return or payoff will be seen in the fulfillment of the promise in your life.

Tom Martincic, in his article, "Gifts and Callings for the Kingdom," stated, "When YAHUAH created Adam and Eve from the dust of the ground, He didn't just sit them in a glass case and say, 'Look at what I did!' He created them to accomplish something; to take dominion over and subdue the earth, to tend the garden and to keep it: to be fruitful and multiply. He had a vision for them."[6]

---

[6] https://www.eliyah.com/kingdomcome-gifts.html

What is your gift? What is your talent? What are your abilities? One of my services to God in His Kingdom is to teach. It would be remiss if I did not do so, for I am a steward of the story of YAHUAH. I am a Light Bearer. It is not my assignment to give knowledge and information but rather to reveal the truth. You might have the ability to teach as well, with such an anointing that the learners are enlightened and able to see things through your teaching that were not visible to them before.

Perhaps, God has placed within you the ability to understand finances and the concepts and principles for creating wealth. Those of you who have seen yourselves managing large sums of money most likely have an aptitude to handle that type of wealth. Your character is invariably trustworthy. You can be trusted not to amass excessive for yourself, unlike Judas Iscariot, the betrayer of Yahusha, of whom the Bible says had the purse for the LORD's ministry but stole from the treasury. Many ministers, like Judas, treat the tithes and offerings according to their will. They steal from the treasuries, church food banks and use the ministry's credit for themselves.

Some people would love to have great wealth, but they are not able to handle it. They do not have sufficient competencies in the world of business and finance. Others have not the sufficiency in their character to deal with the wealth of the Kingdom. If the LORD's gift within you is to manage His affairs, be diligent in allowing the Holy Spirit to develop a Godly character within you.

Notice the response of the two productive servants in Yahusha's parable. Their reactions and rewards should serve as a great lesson for us. These men properly valued and stewarded what had been given to them. They treated it as if it were the master's possessions and not their own. Afterward, they had great reverence because their responses proved how much they valued the master. Just as we see in this example, we have been given the authorization and bounty of grace to use our Master's resources for His glory. Our reactions to this awesome task bear witness to how we see God and what we think about Him. However, **many of us covet the promise and the resources** as if we own them. We say things like *my church, my money, my ministry, and my employees*. When we take care and treat the promises of God as if they are both His and ours, a divine synergy comes into play. **The assignment of God must become so precious to us that we dare not error.**

When we endeavor to be productive and to be the best in His service, the Father, in turn, enlarges our capacity to receive more. For example, when the two productive servants' works were inspected, each of them received more. Yet, when we misallocate and misappropriate God's possessions as the third servant did, our realities will lack quality expectations and rewards.

Misunderstanding purpose for gifts, talents, abilities, assignments, and promises from God will most likely cause us to respond like the servant who was given one talent. He disregarded and disrespected both the commodity as well as its purpose. In my opinion, sometimes, the gifts and callings of God are treated as if they are trivial. It is painful that some servants can be so dismissive to treat the blessing as optional. How many talents, gifts, and promises have been left unused in many vessels? Late Dr. Myles Munroe observed and said that the cemetery is one of the richest places on the planet. It is filled with books that were never written, songs that were never sung, and businesses that were never opened. I admonish you not to allow this to be your testimony. When the opportunity arises to do what you were called to do, seize the moment. Move with dispatch!

In the book of Numbers, the children of Israel got to a challenging juncture where they were delayed for thirty-eight years before entering the Land of Promise. When Moses and the Israelites moved from Hazeroth and camped in the Wilderness of Paran at Kadesh-Barnea, twelve spies (one from each tribe) were sent to explore the Promised Land. Their reconnaissance mission lasted forty days, and they returned with reports and evidence of the Land's abundance. Additionally, however, they retorted the overwhelming power of its inhabitants. Ten of the spies recommended not entering Canaan, but Joshua and Caleb encouraged Israel to enter and take the Land, trusting that God would give them victory.[7] Each of the responses of these twelve men was a testimony of their conception of God. Your response and reaction to your appointment will be a witness for or against you and expose what you really think of the Father.

In the Kingdom of YAHUAH, there is a perpetual cycle of giving and receiving. In Malachi 3:10, we see God challenging Israel to bring their tithes into the storehouse. If they heeded the challenge, He would reciprocate by opening the windows of heaven and pouring out magnificent blessings. When God makes us a promise, we must respond correctly by determining that we will give back a return on the investment that He so graciously promised. Then the cycle continues.

---

[7]Numbers 12:16-14:9 - http://www.ancientsandals.com/overviews/kadesh-barnea.htm

He will give us more responsibilities because *"to everyone who has, more shall be given, and he will have an abundance"* (Matthew 25:19).

The Principle of Giving

Give, and it will be given to you;
good measure, pressed down,
Shaken together, running over,
they will pour into your lap.
For by your standard of measure it
will be measured to you in return.
Luke 6:38

This is one of the most quoted scriptures in the Christendom. It has been taught in Christian meetings all over the globe. It is laced with the most dynamic principle concerning giving. Although inferences are made mostly to money, its implication far exceeds monetary contributions. Unfortunately, some preachers, teachers, and evangelists apply this verse only to the hopes of being financially successful if one pays their tithes or "sows a seed" into some religious project. Yet this scripture, while kept in context, is about the reciprocity of mercy. However, I do trust that there is a principle of interchange in the universe.

Yahusha said, *"Give and it will be given to you."* If we universalize this scripture, we can apply it to many areas of life. Take the giving of one's time to help those in need. It is our humanitarian duty. My husband and I are survivors of the 2005 hurricanes Katrina and Rita. These hurricanes greatly affected the Gulf Coast and rocked the nation. The levees in New Orleans and the surrounding areas broke during Katrina, causing the most massive devastation in modern American history at that time. However, we were amazed at the hearts of the people in our nation and abroad, who poured out so graciously. They gave their time and their substance in an endeavor to help us meet even the most basic of needs. It was by far the greatest exhibition of humanitarianism I have seen up to that point. I believe in God's principle. People that extended themselves to us will receive recompense for their time, energy, grace, and even money. If you give, you shall receive.

We see this principle throughout scripture. In 1 Kings 17 we find these words.

Then the word of the Lord came to him (Elijah), saying, "Arise, go to Zarephath, which belongs to Sidon, and stay there; behold I have commanded a widow there to provide for you." So he rose and went to Zarephath, and when he came to the gate of the city, behold a widow was there gathering sticks; and he called to her and said, "Please get me a little water in a jar that I may drink." And as she was going to get it, he called to her and said, "Please bring me a piece of bread in your hand." But she said, "As the Lord your God lives, I have no bread, only a handful of flour in the bowl and a little oil in the jar and behold, I am gathering a few sticks that I may go in and prepare for me and my son, that we may eat and die." Then Elijah said to her, "Do not fear; go, do as you have said, but make me a little bread cake from it first, and bring it out to me, and afterward you may make one for yourself and for your son. For thus says the Lord God of Israel, 'The bowl of flour shall not be exhausted, nor shall the jar of oil be empty, until the day that the Lord sends rain on the face of the earth.'" So she went and did according to the word of Elijah, and she and he and her household ate for many days. 1Kings17: 8-15

It must be surmised that if the widow of Zarephath had not given the little she had to the prophet, she and her household would not have received such blessings. Instead, they most likely would have died. Her life was certainly blessed because of her obedience and her willingness to give. However, do not miss or overlook an obvious truth. The principles that the Father has set forth do not work solely for those who trust in Elijah's God or who have received Yahusha as their LORD and Savior. This woman was a worshipper of Baal. She did not acknowledge YAHUAH as the "All-Sufficient

One." Yet she received His provision because she gave to the Man of YAHUAH.

Interestingly, one of the connotations for the word *give* in Greek is to *pour out*. The book of Luke expatiates on this topic;

> *Give (pour out), and it will be given (poured out) to you; good measure, pressed down, shaken together, running over, they will pour into your lap. For by your standard of measure it will be measured to you in return. Luke 6:38*

The widow poured out flour and oil to make bread for the prophet. The promise was, if she provided for the Man of YAHUAH, her bowl of flour would not be exhausted, and her jar of oil would not be empty until it rained. She gave flour and oil and received enough flour and oil for her and her son to survive. She was able to keep pouring because she poured out for the Prophet Elijah.

Luke 6:38 gave an agricultural analogy. It was a situation where wheat sellers would measure out the grain. The methods that these suppliers would use were, at times, quite forceful. They would take a basket and pour in the wheat, shake it and compact it to allow more wheat to get inside of the basket. It showed how much they value a good crop or harvest season.

They would pour out a good measure, press it down, shake it together to get the air out, and then pour more until the container would run over.[8] It was analogous to Psalm 23, where King David's cup runs over. But do you see the fine print? "For by **your** standard of measure, it will be measured to you in return." This means that the manner in which you give will be the manner you receive in requital. Whatever measuring standard you use is the same method of measurement that will be used towards you. Positive or negative. In 2 Corinthians 9:6-8, Paul put it this way:

"He who sows sparingly shall also reap sparingly; and he who sows bountifully shall also reap bountifully. Let each one do just as he has purposed in his heart; not grudgingly or under compulsion; for God loves a cheerful giver. And God is able to make all grace abound to you, that always having all sufficiency in everything; you may have an abundance for every good deed."

In other words, "give, and it will be given." If you have the ability to pour out a gallon measure, but you only pour out eight ounces, would it not be futile to think that you shall receive a gallon return? Or if you

---

[8] Ellicott, C. J. (1897). *A New Testament commentary for English readers*. (London: Cassell and Co.)

have eight ounces and you only pour out a tablespoon or even a teaspoon, you will not receive an eight-ounce return.

My friend, you must understand that what you give, how much you give, and the manners in which you give are all important to the Father. Remember, the widow had no problem giving Elijah water, even though there had not been any rain in three years. Her issue was with giving him bread. I am of the opinion that she had more water than food. It is human nature not to give our last or our all, but to reserve some things for ourselves. But our Redeemer, Yahusha Ha'Mashiach, gave His all when He gave His life. He held back nothing, and He is receiving an immeasurable and unending return on His investment.

There is another implication of the word "give" in Luke 6:38. It means to give over to one's care, to entrust, or commit.[9] This is what the Father has done in giving us His promise. He is committing it to your care. He is entrusting you with the gift. So would it suffice to say that, if the LORD has given you a gift, like the owner of the talents, He is expecting a return? Surely He does nothing in vain. In fact, He gives bountifully. So much so that He does not reveal to us the full vision

---

[9] http://classic.studylight.org/isb/view.cgi?number=1325

of the promise at once. He only provides for us a foretaste and according to our capacity par time. What He has in store is so magnificent that you could not handle seeing them all at a time.

Apparently, the principle of giving has a long seam that is sown throughout the scriptures. When God makes us a promise, we must respond correctly by determining that we will reciprocate with a return on the investment that He so graciously promised. Then the cycle continues because He will then give us more responsibilities; to whom much is given, much is required.

The Principle of Fear

From different accounts in the bible, we find many cases where the people of God faced great challenges. Some were internal and personal. However, some challenges were caused by external sources.

One major obstacle that many in the Bible faced was that of fear. In some cases, this gripping emotion may have come with greater or lesser intensity, but very few escaped the trial. Most often, at the genesis of every Rhema from God, there is a sense of fear. It is my opinion that fear is a universal response when one is summoned to approach something greater than. The feeling of being overwhelmed is a typical reaction to

ELOHIYM's beckoning. God is awesome! How could one not be awe-struck when He speaks?

MOSES

> *And the Lord said, "I have surely seen the affliction of My people who are in Egypt, and have given heed to their cry because of their taskmasters, for I am aware of their sufferings."*
> *Ex 3:7(NAS)*

> *Therefore, come now, and I will send you to Pharaoh, so that you may bring My people, the sons of Israel, out of Egypt. But Moses said to God, "Who am I that I should go to Pharaoh, and that I should bring the sons of Israel out of Egypt?"*
> *Ex 3:10-11(NAS)*

> *Then Moses said to the Lord, "Please, Lord, I have never been eloquent, neither recently nor in time past, nor since Thou hast spoken to Thy servant; for I am slow of speech and slow of tongue".*
> *Ex 4:10(NAS)*

> *Moses begged, "Lord, please send someone else to do it."*
> *Ex 4:13 (CEV)*

Moses gives us the perfect illustration of the fear factor. When he encounters the True and Living YAH, his rebuttals were not unfounded. Although he was an

Egyptian prince, he had a speech impediment. In the Torah, Exodus 4:10 records Moses' resistance thusly, *"Please, O Lord, I have never been a man of words… I am heavy of mouth and heavy of tongue."* We have often interpreted this to mean he was a stutterer. While it is unknown exactly what the impediment was, he considered it a sufficient reason to be disqualified for the assignment.

Moses' response is typical of many whose destinies are designed to shake things up, be it politically, socially, and even spiritually. Like Moses, these world changers often make excuses as to why they cannot do what God desires to do through them. They are excited that the Father has chosen them, but on the other hand, they are petrified. I know ministers who initially denied their calling. As if denying the truth negates the mission or the promise.

As for Moses, His reason for not wanting to go back to Egypt was not unfounded. He knew Pharaoh, personally. He grew up in the same household as Pharaoh. He knew his temperament and just how harsh and cruel Pharaoh could be. Moses was well aware of Pharaoh's splendor as well as his armament. Not only did he know Pharaoh, but he also knew the relative nature of the children of Israel. These were judgmental, cantankerous, wishy-washy, complaining people. After he had saved the life of one of their brothers, they immediately turned on him. Is it surprising why he would be more than inhibited about going back to Egypt to deliver the people of YAHUAH?

While Moses knew Pharaoh and the disposition of the people of Israel, He did not know the God of his fathers. He did not know YAH, who would show him what great power was. Hence the following question:

> *And Moses said unto God, Behold, when I come unto the children of Israel, and shall say unto them, The God of your fathers hath sent me unto you; and they shall say to me, what is his name? What shall I say unto them? Exodus 3:13*

Moses was inquiring of God, "What is your name?" The Hebrew word for name, here, is *shem,* which connotes fame or reputation[10]. In essence, Moses was asking God, "What is your reputation?" "What are you famous for?" "What shall I tell the people about you?" Heretofore, the major, notable miracles that had taken place were creation, the flood, and Abraham and Sarah had Isaac in their old age. At that time, there

---

[10] *Brown, Francis, 1849-1916. (1996). The Brown, Driver, Briggs Hebrew and English lexicon: with an appendix containing the Biblical Aramaic: coded with the numbering system from Strong's Exhaustive concordance of the Bible. Peabody, Mass.: (Hendrickson Publishers)*

was no parting of the Red Sea or manna from heaven. Prior to Moses' encounter, God had revealed Himself to Abraham, Isaac, and Jacob as *EL SHADDAI*, GOD ALMIGHTY, All-Sufficient One, or the All-powerful One. But during the time of Israel's enslavement, no signs or wonders had taken place. Though, there was the magic of the Egyptian sorcerers. In fact, the Egyptians worshiped many gods. But the ALMIGHTY GOD had been silent and seemingly void of activity for 430 years.

In her article, "The Names and Attributes of God – El Shaddai," Reverend Linda Smallwood reveals, "*dai,*" which means sheds forth, pours out, or to heap benefits, suggests provision, sustenance, and blessing. Therefore, God is All-Sufficient and All-Bountiful (Genesis 42:24-25). *Shad* or *Shadayim,* which means to overpower or to destroy, suggests absolute power. In the name *Shaddai*, God reveals Himself as the God who compels nature to do what is contrary to itself. He is able to triumph over every obstacle and all oppositions. He is able to subdue all things to Himself."[11]

In my opinion, this explanation of God would have been sufficient to report to the Israelites. I would have gladly informed them that He is the God who pours

---

11 Smallwood, Reverend Linda. "The Attributes of God," http://www.myredeemerlives.com/namesofgod/el-shaddai.html

out His blessings bountifully. He has absolute power within Himself. He controls nature, and He's able to annihilate their enemies—what an awesome report.

However, God did not want Moses to give this report of His fame. Instead, He reveals another attribute of Himself to Moses.

> *And God said unto Moses, I AM THAT I AM: and he said, Thus shalt thou say unto the children of Israel, I AM hath sent me unto you. Exodus 3:14*

The Torah renders this Divine Name of God thusly, I Shall Be As I Shall Be, which in Hebrew is YAHUAH. This signifies that whatever God deemed the Israelites would need, He would Be That! He said to tell them I Am That I Am. Let them know that I AM sent me unto you.

As a bible student, I have found that apart from Yahusha the Messiah, Moses did more miracles than anyone in the Bible. I tend to believe that it is because of this Name that he was instructed by God to wield. Yahusha professed that He is the I AM, thereby showing forth many signs and wonders.

ABRAHAM

Abraham is yet another great patriarch that exhibits fear.

> *After these things the word of the Lord came to Abram in a vision saying, "Fear not, Abram: I am thy shield and thy exceedingly great reward. And Abram said, Lord God, what wilt thou give me, seeing I go childless,"*
> *Genesis 15:1-2 (NKJV)*

Some theologians say Abraham's fear was a result of his experience from previous chapter. He went to rescue his nephew Lot from Chedorlaomer, king of Elam. This king and his allies defeated the twin cities of Sodom and Gomorrah, took all of their goods, food, supplies, and many of the people who lived there, including Lot with his possessions. So, it is believed that Abraham feared reprisal. However, we shouldn't have expected an admonition not to fear if he was actually not afraid of something.

I am of the opinion that Abraham was afraid that his time was running out. What God had promised him was taking an awfully long time to come to pass. I base this belief on Abraham's immediate response.

> *And Abram said, "O Lord God, what wilt Thou Give me, since I am childless…"*
> *Genesis 15:2*

In my observation, Abraham's fear was from the fact that time was running out. In spite of the LORD's encouragement that He would ensure Abraham's reward would be great, yet Abraham experienced the "but LORD" syndrome. The fear of lost time is possibly one of our greatest obstacles. But we must never forget that on the fourth day, according to Genesis 1:14, God created time. Time is not an obstacle or an issue for Him but rather an opportunity. In Isaiah 46:10, He reminds us that He "declares the end from the beginning." His purpose for you has no statute of limitation.

Fear can be one of your greatest enemies. It is petrifying. However, you must learn to press through your anxieties. In the bible, it is observed that the phrase "fear not" appears about 80 or 140 times. A few of the reasons that this emotion has such a tight grip is because:

1. *We fear that we will fail.*
2. *We fear what others will say or do.*
3. *We know that we are not completely capable of doing this thing that God has shown us.*
4. *We feel that we are not worthy of doing such a great thing for God.*

This is a great tension we've all experienced. For some, they are still trying to figure out why they feel that way. The degree to which God wants to work through you haunts you, and you cannot understand how this could be, especially in light of your deficiencies. You think perhaps God made a mistake. How can you do such great exploits for Him? If you are not careful, this dilemma could keep you from ever moving forward. *Someone called this the paralysis of analysis.* Like Moses, without even being cognizant of it, your actions are asking God to get someone else to do it.

Gideon

This leads us to our final example of one who also encountered the fear factor.

> *And the angel of the Lord appeared to him (Gideon) and said to him, The Lord is with you, O valiant warrior. Judges 6:12*
>
> *And the Lord looked at him and said, "Go in this your strength and deliver Israel from the hand of Midian. Have I not sent you?" And he said to Him, "O Lord, how shall I deliver Israel? Behold, my family is the least in Manasseh, and I am the youngest in my father's house." Judges 6:14-15 (NAS)*

The Gideon spirit, as I like to call it, is still prevalent in Christendom today. Further in his account, he did something that so many of us tend to do at some point on this journey of destiny. We ask God for a sign. *"Lord, if this is what you want me to do, then please, give me a sign."* Both Gideon and Moses had to receive signs from God. God did give them a sign, but He also says to you and to me what He said to Gideon, "Go in this your strength." What strength? Gideon felt powerless. He had no power within himself. But the Angel of the LORD told him to "go in ***this*** thy ***strength***." ***This strength*** or might is the truth that "the LORD is with you." It is in this truth that your confidence must lay. The LORD encouraged both of these men with the same blessed assurance; He was sending them. This sending implies that they were being commissioned and, therefore, sufficient for the task at hand. Today, we would call this an anointing.

Because of the anointing, when God gives you a task or an assignment, channel your negative fear into the positive reverential fear knowing that you have been sent by the ALMIGHTY GOD.

The Principle of Imperfection

In the Bible, we would clearly see that God promotes people that others would disregard. God does not look at our pedigree, physique, or even our intelligence. Indeed, God does not call the equipped; He equipped the called. Neither our strengths nor our frailties are an asset or hindrance in the things of God. In fact, He knew all about you before you ever got the call. He knows what you are capable of doing. He is quite familiar with your inabilities, incapability, imperfections, and even your strengths. So the promise is not predicated on how equipped you are. The gifts and abilities that lie within you are God-given to enable you to accomplish His purpose for His glory. So why would you hold yourself to some insurmountable standard that you could never live up to?

Allow God to conform you into the image of His Son, Yahusha the Messiah. Allow the transformation to take place. Paul puts it this way:

For whom He (God) foreknew He also predestined to become conformed to the image of His Son (Yahusha), Romans 8:29 (NAS)

Your past and even present state or condition is no surprise to God. All He requires is your positive response to His leading.

Reflecting again on Moses, who offered God every excuse he could to get out of his assignment, he did not realize that it was God who moved his mother to put him in the Nile when he was an infant. It was that same God who synchronized his arrival at Pharaoh's daughter's bathing pool. That same God brought him up and educated him in the arts and sciences of Egypt and the world, all to equip him for his divine assignment. This same God knew that Moses had a heavy mouth or tongue. All of these things would work together for YAHUAH's good purpose to fulfill the prophetic word He had given to their father Abraham to bring them out of bondage.

Chapter 4

THE PATTERN

Make it like this–

And let them make me a sanctuary that I may dwell among them. According to all that I show thee, the pattern of the tabernacle, and the pattern of all the furniture thereof, even so shall ye make it…
Exodus 25:8-9

The Creator is intentionally systematic. Our solar system shows the order, detail, and meticulousness of His mind. The earth, for example, is the third planet from the sun. According to scientists, it is a watery world, wherein two-thirds of the planet is covered by water. Its atmosphere is perfect for sustaining life. Currently, it is the only world known to harbor life. The earth's surface rotates on an axis at 1,532 feet per second. That is a little more than 1,000 mph. Talk about a shift! It zips around the sun at more than 18 miles per second. This is magnificent, considering it is 7,926 miles in diameter. A day is 23 hours, 56 minutes, and it takes 365.24 days to make its orbit. [12] This is just one rock! Scientists tell us that the universe is still expanding. That means from the time ELOHIYM said "Let there be," the universe, in obedience to His word, kept enlarging and unfolding itself because He never gave it a boundary as He did with the waters. The Creator is magnificently strategic.

Imagine what it must have been like for Moses to enter into the presence of YAHUAH, the ALMIGHTY GOD, and be allowed to come into the sanctuary of heaven. This must have been breathtaking. Upon seeing ELOHIYM, high and lifted up, Isaiah exclaimed, "Woe!" While this was a passionate sigh of grief, Isaiah had the awesome privilege of seeing glimpses of God. The greatness of His glory is truly indescribable.

Moses was taken on a tour through the wonders of heaven's worship center. The place where the angels cry "Holy, Holy, Holy is the LORD of hosts." However, the purpose of his tour was to view and study the design of the Throne Room for the construction of the Tabernacle. This edifice would be where God would dwell among His people on the earth. It is my opinion

---

[12] Choi, Charles Q. "Planet Earth: Facts About Its Orbit, Atmosphere & Size," December 14, 2014, https://www.space.com/54-earth-history-composition-and-atmosphere.html

that the earthly tabernacle was a miniature replica of what is in the heavens. I say that Moses' tabernacle was miniature because, in my child-like imagination, I just believe that everything in Heaven is gigantic.

God charged Moses with making the tabernacle according to the pattern revealed to him while he was on Mount Sinai. YAHUAH showed Moses every intricate detail of this sanctuary from the exterior to the interior. The dimensions were to be specific. The furniture was to be exact. There was no room for error. God ensured that there would be no error by filling the craftsmen with His Spirit of wisdom, understanding, and knowledge in all kinds of craftsmanship. He gave them precision. They were equipped in working with gold, silver, wood, stone, brass blue, purple, scarlet, linen, engraving, embroidery, and weaving. He even called two of them out by name, Bezaleel, the chief artisan, and Oholiab (Aholiab), the artist responsible for preparing the materials for the tabernacle. These men were imbued with the wisdom of God, and He gave them the heart to teach others. They were skilled craftsmen. However, YAHUAH empowered their gifts and overshadowed their understanding of that trade. The LORD is so meticulous that He would give men a special and specific anointing to do what He said, exactly as He said.

How does this pertain to your promise? Here, it is revealed that YAHUAH is a God of order. He is given to exactitude and details. Everything has a purpose. Everything has a place. Everything is for a greater plan than what the natural eye can see and the heart can imagine. This is the truth of your promise. It has a specific purpose in God's Divine arrangement. He must anoint you to do what is assigned to you for His arrangement to be complete. He cannot afford to allow His project to be thrown together or to let you do it the way you see fit. He will not sanction your flesh, permitting it to dictate how things will go or even let you go out ahead of time. The dealings in your life must be according to His Divine pattern.

Bezaleel's name means "under the protection or in the shadow of God."[13] While Aholiab's name means "the tent of the Father."[14] These men were given the enormous task of building the tent of the YAHUAH. As long as they operated in the Divine Will of YAH, the project would be protected and erected without hardship. Moses understood his assignment. The Tabernacle was the place that God had opted to abide with His chosen people, Israel. The severity of the

---

[13] Lockyer, Herbert, "All the Men of the Bible", p.76 (Grand Rapids: Zondervan Publishing House)

[14] Lockyer, Herbert, "All the Men of the Bible", p.42 (Grand Rapids: Zondervan Publishing House)

assignment was in Moses' heart, mind, and spirit. When God gave him the green light, he began the project. But it was not Moses' zeal that got the job done. It was by the Spirit that God made it happen.

This was also the case with Zerubbabel, the prince of Judah. During the time when Jewish exiles returned from Babylon captivity, Zerubbabel was an influential political and religious leader in Israel. Upon returning to Jerusalem, he was subjected to the reconstruction of the temple. The word of the LORD came to Zerubbabel, through the prophet Zechariah, saying the rebuilding project would indeed take place, but it would not be by might, nor by power, but the rebuilding of the temple would be accomplished by YAHUAH's Spirit (Zechariah 4:6).

For the promise to be accomplished, it must be backed by the power of the Holy Ghost. The mission is too great. Too much is at stake for Him to let you do what you have seen without first working some things into and out of your character. Joyce Meyer so appropriately stated, "Your gift will take you where your character can't keep you." It is the task of the Holy Spirit to ensure that we conform to the image of Yahusha, and it is Holy Spirit's responsibility to ensure that you complete your assignment according to the script, which has been written in heaven.

God's economy is nothing like the economy of the world. The world says, be successful, be competitive, get wealth, step on whomever you have to, and make it to the top. But in the economy of the Kingdom, God assigns His resources of wealth and provision to us. He gives us spiritual gifts, talents, and abilities, along with moral and ethical qualities to ensure that we fulfill Kingdom purpose. We are to effectuate the earth for His Kingdom's sake. In this generation, we represent the Kingdom of YAHUAH on the earth. But we must act according to His pattern. There is a pattern in the heavens that must be replicated on earth. Just as Moses' earthly tabernacle was a pattern of what is in heaven, the promised work that you are to perform for God is already being done in heaven. In John 5:19, Yahusha expressed it this way, *"I tell you the truth, the Son can do nothing by himself. He does only what he sees the Father doing. Whatever the Father does, the Son also does."*

In Matthew 16, we read, *"Whatever you bind on earth shall have been [must be what is already] bound in heaven, and whatever you loose on earth shall have been [must be what is already] loosed in heaven."* This is an excellent illumination. "Shall have been," "must be what is already." I suppose that everything that is to "be" is already in the heavens. However, it is our responsibility to be in a position to hear and receive from the LORD by faith and according to His Divine Will, and to carry out what is in the heavenly realm as instructed. Yahusha said, *"The Son can do nothing by himself. He does only what he sees the Father doing, and in the same way"* (John 5:19 TLB). James Burton Coffman states, "Jesus' actions were in full harmony with God's actions, not only regarding their quality but with reference to the manner of their doings."[15] What the Father executed in the heavens, Yahusha replicated in the earth.

As I have previously divulged, God often communicates with me through prophetic dreams. However, He also communicates with me through visions. Often, I would see myself performing some ministerial task before attending a service or going about my day. This was how I knew what I was to do before going on stage to lead worship, to speak, or to witness or prophesy.

One Sunday morning, while preparing for service in my home, the Holy Spirit showed me a vision

---

[15] Coffman, James Burton. "Commentary on John 5". "Coffman Commentaries on the Old and New Testament". <http://classic.studylight.org/com/bcc/view.cgi?book=joh&chapter=005>. Abilene Christian University Press, Abilene, Texas, USA. 1983-1999.

wherein a pregnant woman would come into the area in which I served at the ministry. He instructed me to pray, with specificity, over the mother and her unborn child. It was crystal clear, although He did not reveal to me the face of the woman.

As I worked in my assigned area, about mid-morning, I caught a glimpse of a radiant sister with the biggest, most beautiful round belly walking through the door. She looked as if she would give birth any day. When she came into the room, I was conversing with one of the saints, and I almost missed my moment. But I heard the Holy Spirit say, that's her. Upon sensing His Presence, I fixed my eyes upon her and excused myself from the conversation. I knew her very well. She was active in the ministry. As I gingerly approached her, we greeted one another in love, and I asked if it would be all right to pray for her and the baby? She was more than receptive. As I lay hands on her belly, I began praying all that Holy Spirit had said to me in the vision while looking in the mirror at my home that morning. I began to prophesy to the baby and warned it of what it could and could not do. Holy Spirit showed me that the child was a girl and that she would be prophetic and would see what others could not. He said that she would also be a leader in her generation.

From that time forth, whenever I would see the mother, I would speak to the prophetess in her womb. When the baby was born, her mother brought her to me, and I blessed her. Whenever I see the baby, I would address her as Prophetess. As the child began to walk and eventually run, she would make her way to me; and every time, I would address her as a Prophetess. She relished my announcement of her office. As she grew, her mother would tell me of the things the child would say she had seen.

At the time of this writing, she is already a teenager, a debutant, and a member of several societies in her community, being groomed for leadership in her generation. She's an honorable student with many academic awards. But more than these accomplishments, she is a Seer. To this day, she still responds when I address her as Prophetess! Her parents and teachers are amazed at her wisdom and insight.

What would have happened if I had not been sensitive to Holy Spirit that Sunday morning? What could have been the outcome of the child's life if I had not exercised the gift placed upon me? What might have happened if I had not performed my duty precisely as I had seen it and was instructed in the vision?

Your gift was in the Master's hand even before the foundation of the earth. Paul writes in 2 Timothy 1:9 that we were called with a holy calling before the world began. The promise was made even before creation. Before you came on the scene. Therefore, you must walk according to the pattern of God for your life. Walk according to what you have seen or heard from Him or His messenger.

It is imperative that you are in place and sync with the Creator. Many individuals are functioning ineffectively in offices and even in employment places that they have not been ordained for. David could not defeat Goliath using Saul's armor. That armor was designed to fit Saul. The LORD's pattern for your assignment is specifically designed for you. It is the perfect fit for your personality and disposition. Many, in the Body of the Anointed One, are developed copies of an original. They have patterned themselves after someone else. **You are not a copy**. Your assignment may be similar to someone else's; however, if you listen to the Holy Spirit and do your assignment according to His script, you will experience the blessing. Holy Spirit tells us what the will of the Father is, and to obey is to be a lot less frustrated in the process of becoming who Father has destined us to be. If we fail to do the work according to the pattern of the Father, we are indeed out of order.

Looking again at Moses, if he had constructed the tabernacle according to his own will, he might have made the curtains gray instead of blue, purple, and scarlet. Gray is not a heavenly color. It is an emotionless, dull color. You have heard the term "a gray area." This has the connotation of something being unclear, uncertain, or indecisive. While it has its purpose in the color scheme of God, it is insufficient in the tabernacle.

However, blue is reminiscent of heaven, where the Father dwells. It is the aura of the Holy Spirit and divinity and so much more. Purple is a perpetual reminder of His royalty and majesty, being the eternal King of the Universe. Red is the sacred color for sacrifice and the fire of God. These colors were purposely combined. Therefore, Moses was commanded to build the tabernacle according to the Father's pattern and not his own. Take a tour through the heavens in prayer, and find the pattern for your life, your gift, and your assignment. Then ensure that you construct your promise according to the Father's instruction.

Chapter 5

THE PRECEPTS

I was born to do this-

To this end was I born, and for this cause came I into the world, that I should bear witness unto the truth. John 18:37 (KJV)

Precepts are directives, principles, or commandments for direction, action, and conduct.[16] These rules are not optional; they are mandatory. Therefore, when God speaks, His word becomes law. It cannot be altered or reversed. Isaiah 55:11 reveals the following:

*So shall my word be that goeth forth out of my mouth:
it shall not return unto me void, but it shall accomplish that which I please,
and it shall prosper in the thing whereto I sent it.*

When God speaks, His word always produces fruit. It always accomplishes what He wants to accomplish.

His Divine word will prosper in every place He sends it.

In the beginning, God said, "Let there be," and it was so, and it is still so. Initially, the earth was in a chaotic, void state, but now, it has been recreated by the word. Theologians teach that God created the earth Ex Nihilo or "out of nothing." A careful reading of Genesis 1:2 clearly states that there was water over the surface of the earth, and the Holy Spirit hovered or brooded upon it. However, all of the participants in the process of recreation were prepared to do God's bidding. The Word was there, as said by the Apostle John. Holy Spirit was there, and so was Wisdom, according to Proverbs 8:22-31. Therefore, when the Creator spoke, all that was in His conception became a reality.

Likewise, when He decreed His word concerning you, it became an unalterable reality. It became a law, and both heaven and earth aligned themselves to ensure the mandate was followed. We witness this in the life of Yahusha. In Matthew 8:23-27, Mark 4:35-41, and Luke 8:22-25, the storm was raging, and the disciples, many of whom were skilled, professional fishermen, became fearful that their lives were in danger because of the inclement weather. Upon being awakened by the panicking crew, Yahusha rebuked the wind and the waves, and the storm ceased. Evidently, all of nature adheres to His command.

You have heard men say, "My word is my bond," which means they keep their promises. God's word is His bond. Once He decrees a thing, it must come to pass. According to 2 Peter 3:9, *"**The Lord is not slack concerning His promise....**"* Joshua 21:45 reveals, *"**Not a word failed of any good thing which the Lord had spoken to the house of Israel. All came to pass.**"* Paul said again in 1 Thessalonians 5:24, *"**Faithful is He that calls you, who also will do it.**"* Then the writer of the book of Hebrews said, *"**Let us hold fast the confession of our hope without wavering, for He who promised is faithful**"* (Hebrews 10:23). You were born into the earth to fulfill God's purpose. His word is His bond, and it cannot fail.

YAHUAH's Method of Operation

The Bible contains a simple but yet phenomenal truth. God needs a body! Remember the principles. Whenever God does something in the earth realm, He always works in, with, or through an individual.

In his letter to the church at Colossae, Paul expressly teaches that in Yahusha, all the fullness of Deity dwells in bodily form (Colossians 2:9). Our redemption came by way of our LORD coming in a body. For reasons that are dear to His heart, He is entrusting you with a sacred task as a part of the body.

The Apostle Paul spoke at length concerning the Body of Yahusha in 1 Corinthians 12. God has placed each *member* of the body, where He opted for us to be, for a specific determination. Each of us has a specific gift for a specific call. The promises of the Father are in manifestation, and we are working together for His ultimate purpose.

Take A Look Back

Previously, we discussed how God instructed Abraham, Moses, and Gideon to do certain things to prove to them that they were called to do His bidding. Personally, I have experienced the Father in this dimension. At that time, I did not want to face up to the fact that God had chosen me. I knew I was chosen, but I needed to know for sure. I needed a sign. When God gave the sign, I needed another sign, I would need another sign. Today, I'm just so grateful that God is merciful. When I looked back over my life, all of the signs were there; an identifying thread that had been with me all of my life. As a child, I was a worshipper. I understood who *Jesus* was to me from the very beginning of my cognizance. I sang to Him before I could talk. I used to stand out on our porch and just sing to the top of my lungs to *Jesus*. My audience in those days was the congregation in the cemetery across the street of our house, hence the beginning of the worshipper.

My grandfather, the late Daniel Webster Cotton Griffin, was the Pastor of several churches in Mississippi. I loved going to church with him, sitting on the front pew, taking in every word he would speak. I used to walk around my grandparents' home wearing his hat and shoes, holding his huge Bible, the little preacher. I would climb up into my grandparent's bed with the Bible and preach to the furniture. I was only about 4 or 5 years of age.

My first love letter was, "Dear *Jesus*, I love you; thank you for loving me." I still remember my Father's sister inquiring what I was doing? I informed her with a straightforward 3rd grader's face that I was writing a letter to *"Jesus."* Being an educator, I thought she would understand the importance of this method of communication. But she lovingly stated to me that all I needed to do was get on my knees and pray. Well, I needed her to know that I fully understood that, but I wanted to write Him a letter, hence the beginning of my journaling and, ultimately, author of this book.

I remember Bishop Thomas Dexter Jakes telling how he came upon a dog when he was a child. The dog had just given birth to several puppies, but during the birthing process, she died. Bishop Jakes took those little puppies home with him and poured out all of his mother's dishwashing detergent and filled the clean bottle with milk and nursed the puppies. As a child, God was preparing him to minister to the helpless and the hopeless.

Moses was groomed in the house of Pharaoh to lead, not the Egyptians and the enslaved people but YAHUAH's people, out of bondage and onto the steps of a great destiny. Do you need a sign? Look at your life. I am certain that you will be able to see the pattern of God. Undoubtedly, there would have been events that have taken place in accordance with God's promise. God has been preparing you all of your life for His special purpose. You must have the tenacity of Yahusha to say, *"To this end was I born, and for this cause came I into the world"* (John 18:37) to a people who will ask you who you think you are, or what gives you such rights? Not shrinking back but standing on what God has promised you no matter what!

Where Is Your Faith

> *After these things the word of the Lord came to Abram in a vision saying, "Fear not, Abram: I am thy shield and thy exceedingly great reward." And Abram said, Lord God, what wilt thou give me, seeing I go childless, Genesis 15:1-2 (NKJV)*

> *And He took him outside and said, "Now look toward the heavens, and count the stars, if you are able to count them." And He said*

*to him, "So shall your descendants be."
Then he believed the Lord; and He reckoned
(counted) it to him as righteousness.
Genesis 15:4-6 (NAS)*

Abraham has been called the father of faith. Someone called him the gatekeeper of faith. God counted him as one who was in right standing with Him because of his faith.

To develop true faith, one must be tested. When it seems that your promise will never come to pass, and yet you continue to believe that it will, that is faith. Abraham's faith was not in the promise but in the Giver of the promise. Pastor Shirley Arnold duly noted that if we are not careful, we will make an idol out of the promise. Abraham believed that the promise Giver would be a promise Keeper.

For this reason, his faith in God put him in the right position. The same is true for you because of your faith in Yahusha the Messiah; righteousness has been added to your account with God. By faith, we rightly stand with the Father. Therefore, you are called the righteousness of God in Yahusha the Messiah. Your faith in Him is the greatest asset in your spiritual portfolio. There is absolutely nothing more precious to you than your faith in Yahusha. The Bible says Abraham believed God. He was steadfast. He stood firm on God. Though Abraham believed the LORD, he still needed God to do something. Remember our former observation that many of the people of God faced the same challenges. Here we see that Abraham, like Moses and Gideon, sought God for a sign.

> *Then he (Abram) believed in the LORD; and He reckoned it to him as righteousness. And He said to him, "I am the LORD who brought you out of Ur of the Chaldeans, to give you this land to possess it. And he (Abram) said, "O Lord God how may I know that I shall possess it? Genesis 15:6-8*

Aren't you grateful that God understands? He did not see Abraham's inquiry as one of doubt. He knew that Abraham was trying to attain and embrace all that was being revealed. Abraham believed God, but he, like you and I, wanted to know just how God was going to make His promise come into reality. Abraham's faith in God did not waver. Irrespective of our faith, it is also important to work; faith without work (corresponding action) is dead (lifeless) {James 2:17}.

> *And He said unto him, "Take me a heifer of three years old, and a she goat of three years old, and a ram of three years old, a turtledove and a young pigeon." And he took unto him all these and divided them in the midst, and laid each piece one against another: but the*

birds divided he not. And when the fowls came down upon the carcasses, Abram drove them away. And when the sun was going down, a deep sleep fell upon Abram and, lo a horror of great darkness fell upon him. Genesis 15:9-12 (NKJV)

God told Abraham to bring (take) Him the sacrificial offerings. I am amazed at the way the LORD responded to Abraham. He responded to Moses and Gideon in practically the same manner. He asked Moses, "What do you have in your hand? Throw it on the ground" (Ex. 4:2-3). The Angel instructed Gideon, "Take the meat and the unleavened bread and lay them on this rock and pour out the broth" (Judges 6:20). Now He tells Abraham to "take (bring) me a heifer of three years old." God is not a God who will not go to extremes for those whose hearts are sincere towards Him. He says, "You bring me what you have, and I will show you some of what I can do with it."

As we mature in the things of God, it becomes evident that some of the signs that we once needed to see, at one point in time, become unnecessary. In each of the cases we have discussed, these men were in their initial phases of a relationship with God. When they asked Him for a sign, He did not rebuke them, but rather He obliged them. Why? I believe it is because

He understands what we need for confirmation. Unlike that generation of vipers that Yahusha chided, stating, *"An evil and adulterous generation seeks for a sign"* (Matthew 12:39), God's children differ from them. These people were not of a pure heart. They wanted to see some kind of magic. But Abraham, Moses, and Gideon wanted His confirmation. After receiving a revelation, you do not hear of them ever going back to ask God, "Now, how are you going to do this again? Could you send me another sign?" No! They developed a level of maturity in the things of God, and subsequently, He would give a command, and without hesitation, they moved. This was also true of Yahusha. He, although He is God the Son, never sought the Father for a sign for Himself but purposely for those who did not believe that He was the Son of YAHUAH.

Trust that the Father has given you all that you need to accomplish His mission. Whether they are personal attributes or characteristics, a particular disposition, past training, or even supernatural impartations, they have been given to you on purpose for your assignment. It could be that they are yet to be perfected, but He has deposited every good and perfect gift that is required to fulfill His destiny within you.

Chapter 6

THE PROCESS

Things you must do before you get the promise-

At that time the Lord said to Joshua, "Make for yourself flint knives and circumcise again the sons of Israel the second time." Joshua 5.2

You now understand, and you are even more grateful that the Infinite did not wait for you to get into a particular position or acquire a certain status before He made you the promise. He did not even wait for you to stop or start to do certain things before He affirmed His work in you.

By whatever means the Father has revealed His promise to you, you now have a better understanding that the gifts and calling of God are indeed irrevocable (Romans 11:29). It is possible that you will lose talent. For example, I have known people who had a great vocal ability, after years of misusing their bodies or because of some sickness or disease; their singing ability was lost or removed. But your spiritual gift and the invitation of God can never be removed. The scripture infers that ***there is no change of mind in HIM.***

Are you waiting with great expectation for the Father to manifest His promise? When you sit down for a meal, does it cross your mind? Do you lie awake through the night thinking and praying for it to come to pass? Have you, like Mary, the mother of Yahusha, pondered about the promise in your heart? You may have begun to keep your thoughts to yourself because you fear that others will not receive you. HAVE YOU SEEN IT? Or is it still a mist in your mind? If you have the vision, hold on to it. Allow it to ignite your faith. Trust that the promise of ALMIGHTY GOD will come to pass.

Now, you are on the brink of a breakthrough. You are on the edge of excitement. You are ready to see this great manifestation come to pass. You are indeed in anticipation, awaiting your harvest and your blessing, and indeed looking forward to newness. Like Abraham, God has allowed you to preview what He has promised you, and you gladly receive and accept this great gift of promise that He has made, eagerly expecting it to be fulfilled.

In dealing with the process of obtaining the promise, it is necessary that we are more assiduous in our presentation. Contrary to our belief, there are certain things that we must do before we see the manifestation of God's promise.

To begin this segment, we will look at the Abrahamic covenant, which has lasted through the annals of time. This covenant has extended unto this present age and will last until the Yahusha returns.

This promise or agreement was to make Abraham the father of many nations, hence the changing of his name from Abram to Abraham. The LORD promised to make him exceedingly fruitful and that nations and kings would come from him. ELOHIYM made an everlasting covenant and promised lasting possessions. Ultimately, the Father decreed that He would be a God to Abraham and his descendants. Remember the principles. God made an everlasting covenant with Abraham. Just as the great "let there be" commands in Genesis chapter one, YAHUAH's covenant with Abraham is everlasting. Abraham lived more than 400 years before Moses and the law. His promise went down through the chronicles of times, from Abraham, to Isaac, to Jacob, to the children of Israel, to you, to me, and to the generations to come. It is this association that blesses us.

Dr. Myles Munroe once stated, "God is sovereign until He speaks." The sovereignty of God epitomizes His ability to exercise His will or authority. However, when God speaks, His word becomes law. For this reason, He reports in Isaiah 55:11, "So shall My word be that goes forth from My mouth; It shall not return to Me void, But it shall accomplish what I please, And it shall prosper *in the thing* for which I sent it."

God's word is His command, and He never alters His commands. Yahusha tells us in Matthew 5:17 that He didn't come to destroy the law but to fulfill it. The Father's word is His bond. Once He decrees a thing, it must come to pass.

Several years ago, the LORD ministered to me as I was praying concerning a particular promise He had revealed to me. I prayed for years, asking Him when He would do this thing that He had shown. I understood the magnitude of it and did not want it for myself but for His name's sake. I even felt like I would rather just die if I could not do what He had shown me. Afterward, He informed me that I was not yet ready for the fulfillment of His promise. Needless to say, I was floored by His revelation. I found myself not believing Him. I was ready. His promise was all I could think about. I could sense its closeness. What was I supposed to do? I had faith. I reached up when the preacher would say, "Reach up and get it." I danced for 25 seconds for it. I ran around the church for it. I took three steps into it. It was prophesied that I would get it. I sowed the seed to get it. I did everything church folk were told.

But the Father told me as I prayed that morning that I was not ready. At that time, He instructed me to tell His Body that many of us are awaiting His promise, but we have not yet prepared ourselves to receive from Him. It was disclosed that there are things we must do before we get the promise. What? For many years I thought that God would drop His blessing into my lap because I had faith. All I had to do was wait on His timing. I thought it would be an effortless event on my part. Then I remembered the Proverb.

My son, if thou wilt receive my words, and hide my commandments with thee; So that thou incline thine ear unto wisdom, and apply thine heart to understanding; Yea, if thou criest after knowledge, and liftest up thy voice for understanding; If thou seekest her as silver, and searchest for her as for hid treasures; Then shalt thou understand the fear of the LORD, and find the knowledge of God. For the LORD giveth wisdom: out of his mouth cometh knowledge and understanding. He layeth up sound wisdom for the righteous: he is a buckler to them that walk uprightly. He keepeth the paths of judgment, and preserveth the way of his saints. Then shalt thou understand righteousness, and judgment, and equity; yea, every good path.

Proverbs 2: 1-9

I began to search the scriptures because out of His mouth comes knowledge and understanding. Yahusha expressed it this way, in His conversation with Satan, "Man shall not live on bread alone, but by every word (Rhema, command) that proceeds out of the mouth of God" (Matthew 4:4).

I knew that in the Word of God, I would find the answer to how we are supposed to prepare ourselves because God is the God of Order. With the leading of the Holy Spirit, I have found some interesting truths in the Word that are a major part of the process of preparing for the promise.

Many of you can wrap your minds around, preparing for things from a natural stance. When my husband, Mark, sent me away from New Orleans when the threat of hurricane Katrina was upon us, my car was already prepared for the trip. Why? Because during the year, he would ensure that my car was serviced, that the state mandated tags were up to date and every other function was intact. The gas tank was already filled with gasoline. He had already bought new tires to replace the ones with signs of wear and tear. I cannot tell you the number of vehicles that were stopped in the middle of the road, holding up traffic, because the owners of the vehicles were not prepared for the trip. If God made you a promise, He would ensure that you are spiritually prepared to be an effective witness in His plan.

Now, there is an important aspect of our journey that many do not pay attention to. This is an area of our spiritual walk that separates the audacious from the cowardly. Many do not teach this, possibly because they believe it is archaic or not relevant. They dare not tread these waters. Instead, you are told that all you have to do is plant your seed and believe, not God, but believe that you will get the blessing of God. All you need to do is name it, "call those things which be not as though they were" (Romans 4:17), or sow some seed to get it. Note that in Apostle Paul's words, it is God who calls those things that be not as though they were. This is not to say that He has not empowered us to do the same. However, remember what we discussed in the previous chapter, whatever you bind or loose on earth must already have been bound or loosed in heaven. If we are calling things that are not in His Divine Will, is it any wonder why we have not seen those things manifested in our lives? God is not obligated to fulfill any promise except His own.

Indeed, we want the promises from our Father to be fulfilled. We desire to work the works of Him who will send us and do great exploits in His name. We believe that we are equipped to go against all odds for the Kingdom's sake. We have even experienced a foretaste of what is to come. He has allowed many of you to encounter, on a very small scale, the blessing He has in store for you. But what does He require of us?

The Painful Part of the Process

"This is My covenant, which you shall keep, between Me and you and your descendants after you: every male among you shall be circumcised." Genesis 17:10

Remember the principles? In Genesis, we saw that God had instructed Abraham to be circumcised and all of those (family and servants) who were in his household. This was to be a sign of God's everlasting covenant with him. Let it be established that the circumcision was not the covenant. It was only a symbol of the covenant that El Shaddai had made. Some believed that circumcision was indeed the covenant. Paul had to minister to the Jews and the Gentiles concerning this matter. Really, circumcision of the flesh does not make one righteous. It is one's faith in God that makes him righteous. But do not miss this precept. God instituted circumcision for a purpose. It was a symbol of what took place between He and Abraham. It was a symbol of an eternal promise. It was a mark or a seal that identified

Israel as a separate people. Exodus 4:24-25 records God's displeasure with Moses because he did not circumcise his son Eliezer. The word of God clearly states that God sought to kill him. Many believe that God struck him with some illness. But the imperative of this information is that God will not allow His ordinances to be disregarded. God held Moses accountable for the arrangement of the covenant. Matthew Henry, in his *Complete Commentary on the Whole Bible* notes:

He (God) met him (Moses) and probably by a sword in an angel's hand and sought to kill him. This was a great change; Prior to this God was conversing with him and lodging a trust in him, as a friend; and now he is coming forth against him as an enemy. Omissions are sin, and must come into judgment, and particularly the contempt and neglect of the seals of the covenant; for it is a sign that we undervalue the promises of the covenant, and are displeased with the conditions of it. He that has made a bargain, and is not willing to seal and ratify it, one may justly suspect, neither likes it nor designs to stand to it.

God takes notice of, and is much displeased with, the sins of his own people. If they neglect their duty, let them expect to hear of it by their consciences, and perhaps to feel from it by cross providences: for this

cause many are sick and weak, as some think Moses was here.[17]

God would not have made circumcision a requirement if it were for naught. The precepts of God must be adhered to. When His commands are not upheld, He will respond. Note Brother Henry's comment; omissions are sins. Moses was guilty of the sin of omission. Dr. Myles Monroe has rightly stated that many Christians are sincere, but they are sincerely wrong. Unfortunately, we have not searched God's word diligently enough to know His perfect will. Therefore, we only end up prolonging the process.

To further my point, let us look at Israel. The ceremonial procedure of circumcision was in effect while they were in Egyptian bondage. Joshua recorded that "all the people who came out (of Egypt) were circumcised" (Joshua 5:5). However, this evidence in the flesh that revealed that they were separated unto God was neglected during the wilderness wandering. The babies that were born during the wilderness experience were not circumcised as per God's instruction to Abraham. This neglect was such a big deal to God that He called it a reproach because they

---

[17] https://www.christianity.com/bible/commentary.php?com=mh&b=2&c=4

did not continue to observe the covenant. Their action became a disgrace.

Even though God's precepts went unobserved with the birth of the new generation, He still made provision for them. These Israelis were not operating according to the statutes that God had established; yet He took care of them. He still led them by a pillar of cloud by day and pillar of fire by night. He was feeding them manna and quail. Their shoes never wore out. He kept their parents alive for forty years, long enough to nurture them and bring them up in the admonition of YAHUAH, so that they could inherit the Promise.

God has made you a promise. In doing so, He is looking beyond your faults and into the future, seeing what it is that He wills to be done on earth. You are well aware of the provisions that God has made for you. You would not be alive today if it were not for His mighty hand. He has sustained you. Therefore, you must have the great expectation that the promise of God is coming to pass. Unfortunately, this is the avenue where so many of the saints reside. We know that He is YAHUAH YIREH; His provision shall be seen to bring the promise to pass. We rely heavily on His grace and His mercy, as we should. We are sincere in our hearts, and in our minds, we believe God. We know that what He has said is what He will do because of His goodness and provision. *"God is not a man, that he should lie; neither the son of man, that he should repent: hath he said, and shall he not do it? Or hath he spoken, and shall he not make it good?"(Numbers 23:19)*

Much of the preaching today leads you right up to this point, but it fails at its most sincere attempt at assisting you actually to receive the Father's *best*. You are encouraged to trust that God will give you that great promise because He is a Promise Keeper. You are admonished that if you sow a seed, you will receive your promise from God. Many of you have sown much for many years, and God still has not brought His promise into culmination. Please know that I am not condemning sowing seed, remember chapter one? But for many of you, like me, you have left those fired up church meetings, feeling energized and full of faith after you have sown your seed, only to wind up on the perpetual Ferris wheel of expectancy because you know that God has something magnificent for you. But you are unable to attain it. You pray and ask God when He will open up the door so you can move into your miracle. God is still providing for you just as He did for the new generation, but like them, you have not stepped into His Divine will. Why is there no connection between the promise revealed and the promise fulfilled? I believe that the solution to this query can be found in the Biblical records of Joshua (Yahusha).

The Process of Cutting

> *"So Joshua made himself flint knives and circumcised the sons of Israel at Gibeath-haaraloth." Joshua 5:3*

A flint knife in Hebrew means rock or sharp stone[18]. Is it not interesting that YAHUAH would instruct Joshua (Yahusha) to circumcise with a rock? Our LORD and Savior, Yahusha Ha'Mashiach, is The Rock of our salvation. Note that this was not the first occurrence of a rock being used as a surgical instrument. Remember Moses' wife, Zipporah, used a stone to circumcise their son Eliezer (Exodus 4:25). The Apostle John tells us that Yahusha, our Savior, is the Word. He states, "In the beginning was the Word (logos)…and the Word (logos) became flesh (John 1:1, 14)". The writer of the book of Hebrews shared, "For the word (logos) of God is living and active and sharper than any two-edged sword, and piercing as far as the division of soul and spirit, of both joints and marrow, and able to judge the thoughts and intentions of the heart" (Hebrews 4:12). Zipporah and Joshua made knives of stone, HalleluYAH! Only the Rock, only the Stone, only the Word, only YAHUSHA can get in so deep and cut not only the flesh but the soul and the spirit. Surgical instruments can only do but so much. They can only cut the flesh, but they cannot get into the intents of our heart. When we allow Yahusha to infiltrate our lives totally, He will judge our thoughts and cause us to walk uprightly before our Father, which is in heaven. Adam Clarke says this of Yahusha the Messiah in The Adam Clarke Commentary.

He sees all things, knows all things, penetrates all things, and can do all things. He is the ruler of the heart, and can turn it where he pleases. He enlightens the soul, and calls it gently and efficaciously, *when* and *how* He wills.[19]

This, my beloved, is how you were selected for the promise. In Philippians 2:13 (Cepher) we find these words, "For it is ELOHIYM who is at work in you, both to will and to work for His good pleasure".

The Process of Consecration

Joshua named the place where they were circumcised Gibeath-haaraloth, the Hill of the Foreskins. Can you imagine a hill of bloody flesh? Someone has observed that God instructed Joshua to cut the men in their most personal, private, and productive place. In

---

[19] https://www.studylight.org/commentaries/acc/hebrews-4.html

Hebrew, Gibeath is translated as a hill, and Haaraloth is translated foreskin. In focusing on the latter portion of this word Haaraloth, we find that the etymological meaning is more descript than that of the aforementioned. In fact, it means exposed.[20] It has the connotation that something is loosely projected. It is not curtailed and is therefore unconsecrated. The essential object here is that we live consecrated, sanctified, or set apart lives.

In looking at the children of Israel, we see the prime example of a people set apart for God to exhibit His glory through them. This is the purpose of consecration so that ABBA can display His glory in the Believer's life. Please see this. The Israelites were to be a special and distinct nation. He chose them, just as He has chosen you. When you are set apart unto the Infinite, there is no allowance for an un-curtailed or loosely projected life. Living an uncircumcised life is not an option for you, my beloved. It may be an option for one who has not been chosen by Him, for *"many are called, but few are chosen"* (Matthew 22:14). The life of the chosen is a different kind of life. You must operate on a different level or at a higher frequency. Embrace the difference. It

---

[20] AMG International, Inc., THE HEBREW-GREEK KEY WORD STUDY BIBLE (NAS), Lexical Aids To the Old Testament, 1984 and 1990.

does not mean that you are better than anyone else, but your mission is a different mission.

In the armed forces and the federal government, there are all kinds of positions. Some require a special kind of clearance because they are allowed to go into certain areas off limits to the general population. In contrast, others work daily without ever needing access to these special areas. However, each employee or staff must qualify for the position they hold. Contrary to popular teaching, all are not equal in the Kingdom of YAHUAH. However, all Believers must be given to the study of the Word and available to the Spirit.

As God's elect, consecration is not an option. Spending time alone with Him is the best thing that we could ever do for our spiritual life. The time spent in prayer and study, coupled with our endeavor to know Him as He knows us, is imperative. This will create a dynamic love relationship that shows the Father that we can be trusted with His promise.

Yahusha is our Perfect example. Scripture reveals that He would always leave the crowd and the disciples to be with the Father. This is more than just driving and talking to Him. It goes beyond saying a prayer while lying in bed before going to sleep. It exceeds just talking to Him while in the shower;

relationship requires more than that. Consecrating time to be in the LORD's presence is a necessary and critical component to building a relationship. You must learn to worship Him!

From scriptures, we find many cases where the chosen ones spent time in caves or mountains and even in the wilderness. It seems to me that times of serenity are a prerequisite in the life of the chosen. Moses went to the mountaintop several times. Elijah was in the cleft of a rock. David spent time in the fields alone with God, and later in his life, he went into the cave of Adullam.

Contrary to what we have been taught, God took the children of Israel on a 38-year funeral march. You often hear that they spent 40 years in the wilderness, and they did. However, two of those years were spent at Mount Sinai, where they began to get a better understanding of YAHUAH. This was needful because, for 430 years, they were in bondage, being exposed to the pagan gods of Egypt. This is why they were so quick to erect the golden calf (Exodus 32). For you to be an effective witness to God by way of His promise to you, you must get a ***better*** understanding of Him. Preaching and teaching alone cannot do this for you. Only quality time with Him can accomplish this. God wants you to know Him ***better***. He desires that you diligently seek Him. I challenge you to go deeper in your relationship.

The Process of Healing

> *Now it came about when they had finished circumcising all the nation that they remained in their places in the camp until they were healed. Joshua 5:8*

After the Israelites were circumcised, they had to go through a process of healing. Some of you are experiencing the healing process. You have been frustrated with the methods that the Father is using to develop you. Therefore, you do not believe that God is moving you towards His promise. If you are not careful in this space of your emotions, you could become cynical. I encourage you to identify this attitude and know that just because it has not happened does not mean it will not happen.

For many years I worked in ministry, I knew I had been called to do so much more than I was doing. I worked diligently and faithfully, assisting the pastors to achieve their dreams and vision. But there were times when my heart was extremely heavy.

We were taught that God rewards faithfulness, so I desired to know when the LORD was going to reward me? I had sacrificed so much for the ministry and began to think "Ministry" takes much and gives so little in return. During that dark season, I found myself expecting the ministry leaders to make room for me. However, when this did not happen, inwardly, I became disappointed and at times secretly angry because I felt that they knew God had called me but intentionally refrained me from using my spiritual gifts.

Whether this was true or not, only God knows. However, this disposition gave grounds to the enemy, who convinced me that I was intentionally looked over and that my gifts were being disregarded. What I did not understand then that I totally honor and respect now is that the leaders did not call me. It was not their responsibility to help me in any way.

I have a word of advice to those who want to give up or call it quits because things are not going the way you believe they should. Keep it moving! In those dark days, I never stopped working. Although I was the walking wounded, a silent sufferer, and even the walking dead, because I was dying on the inside, I kept it moving. I would cry out to God to move me, to send me to another place, any place, out of the country. As I sought Him for counsel, He ministered this word to me from Joshua 5:9; *"the children of Israel remained in their places in that camp until they were healed."* No matter how I cried, He would not move me. I wore many masks in those days, but I had to remain in my place in the camp where

I had been cut until I was healed. Many were released by the Father to go to other ministries, and some even started their own. Some left and tried to take me with them. But there I remained, wandering rebelliously and meandering on the outskirts of the camp. At that moment, I knew what it meant to be so close to something and yet be so far away.

Years ago, I had to have surgery. After the surgery, the doctors made sure that all of my vitals were normal before they released me. I was sent home to recover and continue the healing process. I could not drive or go to the grocer. In fact, I could barely walk for a few days. All journeys were canceled. I had to go back to where I initially discovered my abnormalities to complete the healing process. The Father has a way of healing you right in the place where the pain was inflicted.

Healing is a process. It took me many years. But during my emotional ordeal, I never stopped consecrating. During those days, I constantly poured myself out before the LORD. I had to always minister to and encourage myself. However, even in those dark days, He would send me a prophet or someone with an uplifting Spirit-filled word. Perhaps many of you have encountered hardships in life and ministry. Your heart has been broken. You have been misunderstood and even taken advantage of.

Perhaps your family and friends have not embraced your gift, abilities, and talents. They cannot see the promise of the business or the ministry work that has been prophesied over you. If your God-given gifts have been accepted and you have a support system, then you are BLESSED.

Whatever categories you may find yourself remember ELOHIYM made you a promise. It takes being overlooked and being mistreated sometimes to appreciate and cherish the Father and what He has for you. In His infinite wisdom, He uses malicious and even evil things to develop our character. It is said that there is no blessing without a break, no crown without a cross, and there is no gain without pain.

The Hebrew word for healed in Joshua 5:8 means 'to be revived.' It also means 'to enjoy life and live anew.'[21] Many of you are frustrated to no end because you have prayed and you have believed the LORD, but seemingly to no avail. You feel you aren't getting closer to the promises of God. At this point, you must do as Abraham did. Believe that you are on the threshold of seeing the manifestation of your miracle. Trust the LORD with all of your heart and do not lean or trust your own understanding, despite what you see. God

---

[21] http://classic.studylight.org/isb/view.cgi?number=02421

has appointed this time of healing for "the eyes of your understanding [heart] to be enlightened [flooded with light]." It is not until a seed is buried that it is in the right posture to grow. You shall see the goodness of the LORD! There will be a revival! You will experience an abundance of joy and newness of life.

I am a firm believer that when the word of the LORD comes to you, and you receive it heartily, your world will begin to turn right side up. This is the purpose of this book. You must receive divine enlightenment for Him to thrust you into the promise. Remain in the camp. Receive God's healing. Allow Him to revive and restore your soul and spirit. The Father has ordained these events in your life for His ultimate purpose of conforming you into the image of His dear Son. Remember the principles. It was not until the new generation of Israelites was circumcised that they received the promise of God. David had to go through drama with Saul for many years before he was crowned the second king of the commonwealth of Israel. Yahusha had to suffer much pain and persecution before He was resurrected with All Power. Allow the LORD to process you.

Chapter 7

THE PARTICIPATION

Just Do It-

For as the body without the spirit is dead, so faith without works is dead also. James 2:26

Again, let's review Abraham's life. Abraham was given the prophetic promise from EL SHADDAI to be the father of many nations. This word of prophecy came when Abraham and Sarah were aged and out of their reproducing stage. At that time, Sarah was in her menopause. So the promise was absolutely unbelievable to her, such that she literally laughed out loud. Naturally, because of their age, they had challenges understanding how YAHUAH would or even could do what He said. They trusted Him to do it, but how?

This is a major matter for many who would believe God to do what is humanly impossible. Often, we tend to get caught in the BUT vortex of believing. It is the, "I believe, BUT how is He going to perform it?" There are many obstacles that would cause the BUT syndrome. We consider circumstances like, 'I do not *have* the resources to make it a reality. I do not *have* a degree. I do not *have* the money. I do not *have* the influence or connections. Like Abraham and Sarah, you just ***HAVE*** to trust the ALMIGHTY GOD.

Another significant issue in the lives of Abraham and Sarah was their lack of patience. I will talk more about this in the next chapter. However, Sarah's impatience made her suggest that Abraham should take her Egyptian handmaiden, Hagar, to be his wife and their surrogate mother. This, as we know, proved to be disastrous.

Taking a closer look at this Biblical account, we see something that should be of interest to us. Despite their age, and despite her infertility, Abraham and Sarah took God at His word, initially. Perhaps they made at least three attempts to conceive a child. However, when conception did not take place in their reasonable amount of time, they began to think God wants them to have a child by some other means **even though His prophecy was specific.** After an attempt, or possibly two, to conceive, it seemed like a good idea to give Abraham a fertile woman.

In retrospect, we see that Abraham and Sarah had to participate in the process. There was no promise of Immaculate Conception as there was with Mary, the Mother of Yahusha. Abraham and Sarah had to engage in intimate activity.

Over the years, I have come to discover a weakness in the teaching of promises made and purposes fulfilled. In contemporary Christendom, when it comes to receiving the promises of God, we are told to sow seed into some ministry or minister, and God will open a door or give us some opportunity. Sometimes prophets forecast that in three, seven, or even ten days, God is going to extend a supernatural provision. This has been taught over the years to the disadvantage of the Body of Messiah. It is imperative that I point out here that whenever Yahusha spoke of sowing seed, He spoke in terms of the Word, not money. However, if God should require that your participation be a monetary gift, by all means, PARTICIPATE in His process.

Many Biblical icons had a major decision to make when approached by YAH or His messenger to do His Divine will. These people stood at a crossroad or in a place of complexity. They had to make a decision. Abraham had to leave his father's house to get to a place that EL SHADDAI would show him. He also had to make a major decision about his son Isaac. God tested him to prove his faith and loyalty. YAHUAH charged Moses to go back to Egypt, the land he had fled from, to lead YAH's people out of slavery.

Yahusha understood that this was and would continue to be a challenge for believers. Consequently, He taught the apostles to pray, "Thy Will be done on earth..." He showed them how to do that perfectly in Matthew 26.

In scripture, we see situations where God commissioned an individual or a nation to walk in greatness, but because of fear and lack of relationship, they struggled in the process. Noah struggled with building the ark because his generation had never seen it rain before. Moses struggled with going to Pharaoh for many reasons. But the excuse he used was his speech impediment. When the LORD's call comes, it is our responsibility to ensure that the vision, promise, or expectation of the LORD comes to pass. But how are we to do this?

Our focal scripture provides for us the indisputable reality that faith alone is not enough. As I alluded earlier, it was always my belief that God would send His promise to me from heaven, and there would be nothing for me to do but receive. James reveals that having faith and doing no work to ensure the promise comes to pass is like unto a body with no spirit or life. We call this death.

For you to see the promise of God, it is expected that you make valuable contributions and sacrifices. This contribution or sacrifice could be of money if the promise calls for some investment. It could be of education, should the promise deem it necessary for you to be cultivated in a certain discipline. You may be required to take some unpopular stance in order to see the provision of the LORD. The requirement may even be the need for you to remove yourself from carnality whether it is found in yourself, someone close to you, or some entity in which you are affiliated. Whatever the prerequisite, ensure that you are prepared for it and that you do it.

When the Father announced to Abram that his descendants would be innumerable, Abram went through what Henry Blackaby describes as the crisis of belief. Whenever God contacts us to work with Him, it always leads us to a crisis of belief that requires not only our faith but also some action![22] God always requires us to do two things. First, to believe Him, and second, to

---

[22] Blackaby, Henry T., Experiencing God: Knowing and Doing the Will of God, Revised and Expanded, 2008.

do whatever He says in the process. Our participation is critical in the course of bringing the promise to pass. John Wesley is quoted as having said, "It seems that without God, man cannot, but without man, God will not." John C. Maxwell said, "Dreams don't work unless you do." In other words, God requires us to act on His word.

The children of Israel could have stayed in Egypt. However, they purposed within themselves to believe the God of their fathers, Abraham, Isaac, and Jacob, and therefore made preparation on the night of Passover to leave. They did all that Moses instructed them to do. Even down to borrowing gold, silver, and jewels from the Egyptians. While God wrought plagues and destruction upon the Egyptians' heads, He did not swoop the people of Israel up in a whirlwind and drop them into the land of promise. They had to participate in the promise. You must hear the word of YAH, take heed to it and then do as He says. In doing so, you will see the salvation of the LORD!

Chapter 8

THE PATIENCE

In His Time-

The end of a matter is better than its beginning; Patience of spirit is better than haughtiness of spirit. Ecclesiastes 7:8

There is one area of utmost importance that we must discuss. It is possibly the most critical point of all, and that it is about **waiting patiently for the promise**. This is the area where most fail. Sometimes, waiting patiently on God can be a long, arduous process. Many shrink back and never see the true blessing of the LORD or His earthly desires fulfilled. James tells us, in his epistle, "the trying of our faith works patience" (James 1:3). Remember the principles. God always tries the elect. The trying method is not to see what you will do. But it is to develop your character and to expand your level of patience. When our faith is tried or tested, our patience is being developed.

What is patience? Patience is the ability to bear something without complaining. It is a peaceful calmness and stability in the midst of a trying circumstance. Patience is one of the nine fruit of the Spirit found in Paul's letter to the Galatian church, which is exhibited perfectly in Yahusha Ha'Mashiach. Patience, longsuffering, or stoicism must be developed in the character of the called. While we can be apprehensive about seeing the promise come to pass, we must reflect confidence and calmness in our emotions. All we need is to believe in the Promise Giver, who is a Promise Keeper.

Taking a page from the playbook of Yahusha, during His three years of actual ministry, we never see Him showing anxiety. According to the Bible, He seemingly was never too eager about anything. Neither was it recorded that He was ever afraid. Some might say He was anxious or afraid in the Garden of Gethsemane. At that moment, Christ is described as being in agony, not anxiety or fear. Except to the Father, the Savior never expressed concern about what would happen. He was never moved by the accolades of the masses or the chidings of His enemies. When His brothers attempted to press Him in John 7:3 to go to Judea, so His disciples could see the Works He was doing, He retorted, "It's not my time." Though being the Messiah, He expressed and demonstrated complete confidence, trust, and dependence in God the Father. Just as Satan had tempted Him in the wilderness, Yahusha's brothers were endeavoring to tempt Him to do what God had not ordained. They said, "Go show the world that You are a Rock Star! You know that you want to go public." Many would have said, "Yes, I'll go and show them who I am. I will hold a tent meeting or a conference, and they will see that I am anointed!" Yahusha understood the timing of YAH! All things ordained by God must transpire in due season, in YAHUAH's own time and in the fullness of time.

Isaiah 46:10 reminds us that God knows the end from the beginning. I have learned that when God speaks, it is already done. We, however, must catch up with that utterance. It is taught that God does not do what He says immediately. It is not the truth. When the Word of God goes forth, it is already done in the realm of the Spirit. However, preparation and manifestation happen in time. It is in time that if we are not careful, we will find ourselves becoming impatient.

Whenever the Father makes a promise of grave proportions, do not look for it to come to pass right away. **The promise is for an appointed time.** There are things that must occur in your life, as well as in history before He can put His gift on display. Sometimes, things must get worse before His solution can come, through you, to make things better. For some of you, your gift cannot be exposed until certain things happen or are set up in the earth realm. This was the case with me. I had no means of reaching the world for Yahusha until the technology was developed for us to live stream and interact with others across the globe. Your gift is greater than you can imagine. You must let patience have her perfect work.

In the New Testament, the word *patience* also means endurance. It carries the connotative characteristic of a person who is not moved or swayed from his purpose by trials and suffering. You have to resolve within yourself that you will wait on the LORD and be of good courage, no matter how long it takes to see the manifestation of His promise.

Many have been waiting for years, but I encourage you, continue to wait. Psalm 27:14 vehemently expresses that we should, *"Wait on the LORD: be of good courage, and he shall strengthen thine heart: wait, I say, on the LORD."*

Remember our discussion about how God's chosen people experienced the same situations? In a previous chapter, we talked about Abraham and his fear; fear that time was running out.

And Abram said, "O Lord God, what wilt Thou Give me, since I am childless..."
Genesis 15:2

Here, we see that the great patriarch is possibly concerned about his age and the age of his wife. This was always an issue with Abraham and Sarah. Surely there were some long days and great journeys between his departure from his kindred in Genesis chapter 12 and this great dialogue between him and EL SHADDAI in chapter 15. Time was passing. Abraham was getting older. He may have felt that time was not on his side. Dr. Martin Luther King, Jr. so amply said that "longevity has its place," and I am certain that Abraham would have agreed, but not in the area of procreation.

I am amazed at this discovery. If we observe this further, we will find that Abraham had already made another provision aside from his son Ishmael. He had made Eliezer of Damascus, heir (the son of acquisition). Considering Abraham's journey, we see that he left Ur of the Chaldeans and went north to Haran. The Bible says that he and his family accumulated and acquired souls (people) in Haran. Then, they went southward towards Canaan (the land of promise). I am certain that they did not only acquire souls in Haran but probably, all throughout their expedition towards the Negev. Surely, people were joining their caravan in search of a better life and greater opportunities, just like today. As they went down south, they passed through Damascus, the birthplace of Eliezer. Chronologically, I see that God made Abraham the promise of being a great nation before he met Eliezer. I am unclear about when Abraham considered Eliezer his heir, but Abraham decided that this person would be his son of acquisition. Although Abraham did not have the extended plan of EL SHADDAI, he determined that the affairs of his house needed to be set in order.

Get the picture. God tells Abraham that he would be the father of many nations. After this great declaration, Abraham made Eliezer the son to whom all of his possessions would be given. Apparently, Abraham had a history of attempting to counter God's plan. His affair with Hagar, producing Ishmael, was not the first. In essence, Abraham says to EL SHADDAI, "I have selected an heir." So often, we attempt to bring God's promise to pass through our own means and methods. Often, we want the Father to work within our paradigms rather than allowing the course of God's time and His constructs to be imposed.

There are many individuals operating out of the will of the Father because He told them what they would do, and they made their interpretation of His vision come to pass. **This is tragic, and it's always**

short of God's perfect will. No matter how good it may be, it is still short of the blessing. No matter how well things are working, it is still unacceptable to God. YAHUAH rejected both Eliezer and Ishmael. **Learn to wait on God**. Learn to be content right where you are while looking forward to and pulling in the promise of El SHADDAI. For me, one of the worse things in Christendom is seeing a person or a church concocting or conjuring something up that God did not conceive. It may have bells and whistles. It may take you to places you never thought you would go. But when it is all said and done, what do you have, a good experience or a life-changing experience? You can always tell what God has put His stamp of approval on. There is nothing else like it. It flourishes and is for the good of others.

Do not hurry in God's process. Wait patiently on Him. You can take what He says to the bank simply because He said it. I have encountered people who exhibit a frantic rage because God was not moving quickly enough. If you are doing all that is required of you, you have nothing to be concerned about. Just learn to submit your will to His Divine will. He is credible, and He can do the incredible. You can bank on Him.

Chapter 9

THE PARTNERS

Divinely Connected-

*Let brotherly love continue. Be not
forgetful to Entertain strangers; for thereby
some have entertained angels unawares
Hebrews 13:1-2*

We are admonished by the writer of the epistle to the Hebrews to continue in brotherly love. Apparently, this admonition was necessary because they were either failing or on the verge of failing in this area. In today's arena of life, it is amazing how we are separated from one another. And this period that I'm completing this book, the entire globe is practicing "social distancing" and wearing masks because of the Coronavirus pandemic. This highly contagious disease is not bringing humanity any closer.

Unlike when I was growing up, we knew practically every person in every house for at least a three-block radius, but now, we barely even know our next-door neighbors. We are suspicious, frightened, and afraid of everyone withholding our love out of fear of being hurt or taken advantage of in some way. This is also true in local assemblies and in politics. We barely trust spiritual leaders, not to mention civic and governmental heads. I find this fascinating because we sit under leadership year after year, but we have no faith or trust in them. To exacerbate this issue even further, many people are in marriages where they hold out in the area of love. Couples refrain from giving their whole self to the marriage due to a delusional, convoluted frame of thinking that their mate might one day leave them for another. Therefore, they are unable to build a fulfilling life together as life partners.

Interestingly, when the LORD began to minister His plan to me several years ago, the promise seemed so far away. But in time, He would teach me a very critical lesson. The scriptures caution us about being careful of the manner we entertain or receive people. We could find ourselves entertaining Gabriel or even Yahusha, Himself, unknowingly. Abraham had a visitation from the LORD in Genesis, chapter 18. It was not an open vision or a prophetic dream; it was a real physical meeting. Theologians call it a theophany, wherein YAH visibly manifests Himself.

I once heard a message preached by Pastor Sheryl Brady about the Stranger. This sermon will forever be on record as one of many that God used for me. At a very crucial time in my life, it gave me clarity and a better understanding of what He was teaching, by His Holy Spirit. It seemed that at that juncture, everything God revealed to me had something to do with the principle of partnership. He spoke through several influential men and women in the Kingdom to confirm this truth. For their expositions, I am eternally grateful. They are truly angels.

I call them angels because they are God sent. The word ***angel*** in the Greek means *"Messenger"*. But it is etymologically derived from a word that means to ***"induce."*** God places people in our lives to assist us with bringing forth what He has placed inside of us. Remember the principles? When God sets a thing in order, it continues until He says otherwise. The principle of partnership is seen throughout the Word of God. From Genesis to Revelation, we see that God works through partnerships. A careful look at scripture reveals that almost every great man or woman in history had someone they were divinely connected to for the achievement of God's plan.

In Scripture, we see several Divine Connections. Ruth was divinely connected to Naomi. Through the wisdom and understanding of the customs of her people, Naomi taught Ruth the methodology of making known her availability to Boaz. Her action attracted Boaz's attention. If not for Naomi, Ruth possibly would not have married Boaz. But God deemed it so, that the lineage of our Messiah would come through the bloodline of David.

Another great example of this reality can be seen in the book of 1 Samuel. Samuel was divinely connected to Israel's High Priest, Eli. Samuel's mother, Hannah, brought him to Eli as a child. He grew up, practically, in the house (tabernacle) of the LORD. Eli taught him the workings of ministry to YAHUAH. It was necessary to God that Samuel would grow up in His house.

And Samuel grew, and the Lord was with him, and did let None of his words fall to the ground. And all Israel from Dan even to Beer-sheba, knew that Samuel was established to be a prophet of the Lord. 1 Samuel 3:19-20

God designed it so that Eli would teach Samuel all of the functions of the priestly order. This was necessary because the purpose of God was to do a new thing in Israel (1 Samuel 3:11). For this to have been accomplished, God ordered a Divine Connection between Eli and Samuel. When the sons of Eli were killed, and Eli died, Samuel became YAHUAH's voice to the nation.

Also, there is a divine connection between Samuel and David. It was Samuel who anointed David, the beloved King of the commonwealth of Israel. This principle of Divine Connection is reflective in the life of Elijah the Prophet and Elisha, his successor. Ultimately, we see this dynamic reality with the twelve apostles who needed Yahusha for them to fulfill His purpose in their life.

Further, let's look at Apostle Paul. Paul encouraged Timothy in 2 Timothy 1:6 to "stir up the gift of God," which was within him. See the principle? Timothy had Paul as his Divine Connection, encouraging him to keep the gift, which was like a fire, kindled. That is what your promise should be like for you, a fire. It must be to you like the brazen altar or the candelabra in the tabernacle and the temple of YAHUAH. God gave the fire, and you must keep it burning. He will make provision for you to receive whatever or whomever you will require to keep it burning! He has ordained someone to be connected to you to assist you with your assignment.

When this truth was revealed to me, I became inspired. From then on, I began to appreciate every individual in my life who has been influential, even in the smallest way. From my childhood until this day, ABBA has connected me with souls who were intricate in my growth and development. The Father has been so gracious to me on this journey of destiny.

In my opinion, this matter of divine partnerships can be compared to the certified professionals in a hospital delivery room. These individuals are there to assist the expecting mother with the delivery of her child. Each of these persons has a specific duty and responsibility, and they are able to do their specific job for the benefit of the mother and her child. However, if there are concerns about the mother's health or her baby's health, her doctor will use medication to ***induce*** her labor. This can be a necessary process when the delivery is being jeopardized. In like manner, the Infinite sometimes works in others to encourage us to press to possess the promise.

You must pray and ask the Father to make you keenly and totally aware of your divine partners. Many are positioned for your developmental stage; this is the LORD's doing. Some have a positive position for your progression, while others have a negative effect. However, they are for your ACTIVATION. Today, we are being encouraged to drop people that are not in line and in step with where we perceive we are going. I caution this action because it could be that they have been ordained of God to prime you for the promise.

Biblically, there are scriptural references to this fact. In 1 Samuel 1:6, there is a man named El'ka-Nah. He lived in the days before Saul was coroneted King of Israel. A polygamist, El'ka-nah had two wives, Peninnah and Hannah (whom we have previously mentioned). Peninnah had children while Hannah had none, so Peninnah flaunted this fact in the face of Hannah daily. However, Hannah might not have desperately sought the LORD for a son if Peninnah did not provoke her. As a result Hannah went into a divine partnership with GOD. Hannah wanted a son, and GOD needed a Prophet. ***He used Peninnah (negatively) to press Hannah into prayer.*** She told GOD, if You give me a son, I will give him back to You all the days of his life (1 Samuel 1:11).

Yahusha's divine connection to Judas Iscariot initiated the crucifixion of the Messiah and brought about our redemption. Had Yahusha expelled Judas from His presence, knowing He was the son of perdition who would betray Him, the epic event could have gone another way.

There will also be individuals of specificity that YAHUAH, Himself, has strategically put into places or positions, some for influence and others for affliction. There are also persons who are tactically postured as gatekeepers, who are awaiting your arrival, such as John the Baptist. Yahusha was in divine partnership with John. He required John for the purpose of declaring and preparing the way of the LORD. We too are in divine partnership to ensure that the LORD's undertaking is executed. However, He has also established that we are connected to others that are intricate in our divine destinies.

Chapter 10

THE PRESS

Get In The Press-

"So let us know, let us press on to know the LORD. His going forth is as certain as the dawn; And He will come to us like the rain, like the spring rain watering the earth."
Hosea 6:3

Previously, I cited Pastor Shirley Arnold, who emphatically said if we are not careful, we might make the promises of GOD an idol. I echo this caution. We must be acutely aware of our heart in these matters. It is imperative that we question our motives. We must ascertain if our desire to do that which we have received from GOD is for the benefit of ourselves or for the good of all.

Press to Know Him

In his biographical summation in Philippians 3, Apostle Paul amassed his legal righteousness and then dispelled it to prove that none of what he did, even for

God, was greater than having the knowledge of the Yahusha Ha'Mashiach. Paul even thought that being an accomplice in the stoning of Stephen, who was also an Apostle of Yahusha, was for God's sake! Whatever we do must directly be related to Yahusha. It is Yahusha who has given us the authority to do great exploits. He promised that if we believe in Him, the works that He did, we would do, and greater, because of His ascension to the Father (John 14:12). There is nothing that we can do or accomplish that can take precedence over our relationship with Yahusha, our LORD.

Paul, in his epistle to the church at Rome, rejoiced when he began to ponder the wisdom and knowledge of God.

> *Oh, the depth of the riches both of the wisdom and knowledge Of God! How unsearchable are His judgments and unfathomable His ways! For who has known the mind of the Lord, Romans 11:33-34*

And yet Hosea admonished the Israelites to do all that they could to get an understanding of the LORD. This, my beloved, is my challenge to you today. Press, pursue, run after, and do all that you can to know the Messiah, Yahusha. It is impossible to have a relationship with someone you do not know. He is alive, so there will always be new things to learn about Him. We can never exhaust knowing Him. Humanly, we can never have an exhaustive understanding of people around us because they are alive, and there will always be new things to discover.

Too many of us have a superficial knowledge of Yahusha. We study scripture, but we have a very limited understanding of the YAH of the scriptures and His Mashiach. Many spend more time talking about Him than they do to Him. What sense does it make for a couple to get married and never take the time or the opportunities to know one another intimately after their wedding day? To receive salvation is wonderful, but to stop just after that is a tragedy. It is of great consequence now that you have received a promise from YAHUAH, to press on to know Him more.

Press into Worship

In this dispensation, I believe that the standards of YAH are being reintroduced. The carefree, cavalier lifestyle that is being exuded throughout the Church of Yahusha, which in my opinion, is a direct link to what is happening in the world. The Father is now calling the TRUE CHURCH to order. He is yet looking for the true worshipers. Please get this. Many have not seen the manifestation of the Father's promise because they are yet to experience true worship. Painfully, it is not absolutely their fault. Most of the preaching and teaching they hear only gets them to a certain point, and it leaves them there to fend for themselves.

Remember the principles? Why would GOD, being so meticulous even about the creation, be willing to accept anything less than pure adulation when it comes to our worship of HIM? Bear in mind that the children of Israel were on a 38-year wilderness journey according to Deuteronomy 2:14. They spent two years being taught how to worship YAH. Those days were vital so that they might learn how to and how not to approach the Almighty. If He was so serious about them knowing Him that He gave a two-year training course or Master class, why then would He accept anything less than true worship today? And let us not forget that many of those who participated in that course failed eventually!

Remember the pattern? Hebrews 8:5 reveals to us YAH's warning about His pattern. Moses was warned concerning the construction of the tabernacle; *"SEE,"* He says, *"THAT YOU MAKE ALL THINGS ACCORDING TO THE PATTERN WHICH WAS SHOWN TO YOU ON THE MOUNTAIN."* If there was no room for error then, there is no room for error now. We are guilty of relying too heavily on the graces of GOD as a means of escaping our responsibility to do what He has outlined in His Word.

In 2 Samuel 6:1-7 and 1 Chronicles 13:9-12, there is a biblical account of a man named Uzzah who was struck down by YAHUAH. He was killed for attempting to protect the Ark of GOD from falling from a cart as David and his entourage transported it from Kirjath Jearim to Jerusalem. Uzzah's unfortunate death was a result of the Ark not being transported as YAH had instructed Moses and Aaron; more than 400 years prior. Although the Ark was on a new cart, this was not the manner in which YAHUAH wanted His Presence to be carried. It was to be elevated on the shoulders of the Kohathites, one of the four priestly divisions of the Levitical order. Their sole purpose was to transport the Ark of the Presence. So, there is no alternative, no grace, and no substitution for TRUE WORSHIP!

In the Greek language, one of the meanings for the word ***worship*** *"is to kiss the hand as a token or sign of reverence."* The analogy is that of a dog who licks the hand of his master. For eating from his master's hand, it is evident the dog is loved, nurtured, and even disciplined. In the New Testament, the act of kneeling or prostrating to show great respect or to make a request often expresses worship.

It is imperative that your life be a life of worship. The challenge with this is that many sincere believers do not truly know what it means to worship the ELOHIYM. From the Greek point of view, worship has nothing to do with the tempo of a musical selection. In ministries today, upbeat, fast, and loud songs are equated with praise. Alternatively, the softer and more solemn selections with minor chord renderings are viewed as worship. Having been a worship leader, I do not dispute this. However, this itself is not worship. The late Dr. Derek Prince describes worship as an attitude. One can only revere another if he or she recognizes that the one being reverenced is worthy or WORTH IT, not by mere acknowledgment but by sincerely and totally embracing it as a fact and even more so a truth. Our attitude must be such that we exclaim with exuberance and sincerity that YAHUSHA is WORTH IT!!!

We can see worship in its purest form in Isaiah 6:1-8. The outline is so clear.

> *"In the year of King Uzziah's death, I saw the Lord sitting on a throne, lofty and exalted, with the train of His robe filling the temple. Isaiah 6:1*

First, Isaiah became cognizant that He was in the very presence of the Supreme Ruler. Without a doubt, He knew that he saw the INFINITE, in all of His majesty and HOLINESS.

Interestingly enough, we can identify with ELOHIYM's greatness because we either know or know of some great people. We can also identify with His goodness because we know some really good people. But it takes divine revelation to wrap our minds around YAHUAH'S HOLINESS fully. As the sages say, totally "Other." It is unlike anything that we are really accustomed to.

Note that Isaiah saw the LORD high and lifted. Can you fathom that we are under the all-seeing eye of the Highest God? Psalm 33:18 says, *"Behold, the eye of the LORD is upon them that fear him, upon them that hope in his mercy."* Psalm 34:15 tells us that, *"The eyes of the LORD are upon the righteous, and his ears are open unto their cry."* The eyes of the LORD are always upon us.

Not only are His all-seeing eyes on us, but His presence is also with us. He surrounds us. The Seraphim cried out, *"The whole earth is full of His glory"* (Isaiah 6:3). Paul exclaims in Romans 1:20, *"For HIS invisible attributes, namely, his eternal power and divine nature, have been clearly perceived, ever since the creation of the world, **in the things that have been made**. So they are without excuse." -Romans 1:20 NIV*. We see His Presence all around us, even in one another, for we were made in His image and in His likeness.

Secondly, Isaiah became cognizant of his sin and the sin of the people while in the throne room.

> *"Then I said, Woe is me, for I am ruined! Because I am a man of unclean lips, and I live among a people of unclean lips:"*
> *Isaiah 6:5*

Here is what hinders most believers in the worship experience. Our sins and the guilt thereof cause an emotion of unworthiness. For many, it is impossible to go before His Holiness after having committed some unholy act. Countless Christians will not even go to a worship service after participating in some sinful act because of the guilt. I implore anyone who finds himself or herself in such a state to Press into the Presence of YAH.

Thirdly, Isaiah received cleansing and forgiveness.

> *"Then one of the seraphim flew to me, with a burning coal in his hand which he had taken from the altar with tongs. And he touched my mouth with it and said, 'Behold, this has touched your lips; and your iniquity is taken away, and your sin is forgiven.'"*
> *Isaiah 6:6-7*

When we press into the Master's Presence, we find mercy, grace, and peace. It is in His Presence that we are cleansed and conformed into the image of Yahusha.

It is in His Presence that the matter of forgiveness of sin is settled.

Lastly, I am a huge proponent of how to respond to Yahusha. Whenever He says or does something, I believe we should respond. It is the same way in the natural. If someone you love tells you they love you, you respond by saying, "I love you, too." In worship, we have the awesome privilege of responding to YAH and to His will. While in the throne room, Isaiah heard YAH ask a question, *"Whom shall I send? And who will go for us"* (Isaiah 6:8 NIV)? Isaiah responded to this query, volunteering, *"Here am I. Send me!"* This must be the response of your heart as a recipient of a promise from Him. We must give the LORD our YES! I will!

Remember we said that worship is an attitude. It is imperative that we properly approach GOD. There is an acceptable way to worship the Almighty. Someone accurately added that True worship is the soul's adoration of the Creator functioning obediently to the Divine Will. Someone has also defined worship as being "the ultimate liberation of the human spirit." When we worship the Father in spirit and in truth, our souls and spirits are at liberty to function within the confines of the Holy Spirit, and these restrictions are actually limitless.

Press Toward The Mark

"I press toward the mark for the prize of the high calling of ELOHIYM in Mashiach Yahusha." Philippians 3:14 (Cepher)

Although it seems that Paul is speaking in eschatological (end time) terms, I would like to take liberty with this scripture and say that your promise is a high calling of ELOHIYM in Mashiach Yahusha. The Father has revealed to you His design for your life, and you must therefore ***press to possess*** it. Your goal is to ***be*** that which He has called you to be. This will require participation on your part. Too often, we expect the Father just to drop the promise in our lap or just make it happen like magic. But there are things that you are required to do. You must participate in the process. In this scripture, Paul's analogy is that of a runner in a race. In the simplest term, if the runner does not run, he cannot qualify for the prize.

When God made Abraham the promise that he would be the father of many nations, He explained to Abraham that his heir would come from his own body. This meant that Abraham would have to participate in the process. Even Sarah would have to participate in the promise of the Father to manifest it. Abraham's promise would not have happened if he and Sarah had not extended and exerted themselves. Sarah had to initially press through doubt her days of reproduction were far spent! It is one thing to be young and barren and then have the LORD give you the promise of a child. However, it is another matter to be up in years when gestation in the womb is scientifically impossible. Is it any wonder Sarah said, "Yeah right," and laughed?

But the promise would call for Sarah and Abraham to *do* something that they may have thought was no longer necessary in their minds because of their age. I am sensing, even now, that some of you have stopped doing some things because you think they are not necessary anymore. You have lost your zeal and enthusiasm. Get back on track! Get in the game! Who told you to quit? This is necessary. The Father has designed it to be a part of your development.

It is factual that the Father works through people. The Bible bears witness to this. He needs your body. This is why Paul tells us to present our bodies as a living sacrifice, well-pleasing to God, which is our spiritual, reasonable, rational service of worship (Romans 12:1). Abraham and Sarah had to ***Press*** past their natural impediments to see the promise come to pass. I challenge you to ***Get in the Press***!

Chapter 11

THE ULTIMATE PROMISE

The High Calling-

I press toward the mark for the prize of the high calling of ELOHIYM in Mashiach Yahusha Philippians 3:14 (Cepher)

As mentioned in the previous chapter, your promise from YAHUAH is a High Calling. GOD has selected you for His Divine purpose. You must settle this in your mind and your spirit. GOD does nothing by happenstance. His actions and plans are very meticulous, and they are of eternal proportions. We see evidence of this, again, in the life of Abraham. Abraham is the father of three relative religious movements, the Jews, the Christians, and the Muslims. All of them call him father Abraham.

Your gift and your promise is a high calling of GOD in and through Yahusha and His Holy Spirit. For some of you, it is of an epic magnitude. Your ministries will reach far and wide. You will touch the lives of millions for Yahusha. It may be through the preaching of the gospel of the Kingdom or some humanitarian deed, or you may be the next great Psalmist. Others may be called of YAH to be the parent or mentor to the next Samuel or Elijah. You may be a business owner and produce some solution that will help millions. Whatever your assignment is, endeavor to remember that you have been chosen by the ALMIGHTY GOD to do His bidding. Therefore, do it heartily as unto the LORD and not unto man (Colossians 3:23).

I dare not sell you the unrealistic hope that you will not be tried and tested before, during, and possibly after your mission. Be assured that His plan is a success because the end was established at the beginning. But I, like Paul, I'm confident of this very thing, that

> ***He who began a good work in you will perfect it until the day of Yahusha Ha'Mashiach*** (Philippians 1:6 Cepher).

Hence, I encourage you with the words of our Mashiach Yahusha from Revelation 2:10 ***"be thou faithful unto death, and I will give thee a crown of life."*** This, my beloved, is the **Ultimate Promise,** that you shall receive a great reward if you remain faithful to GOD until the end. Therefore, in all that you have been assigned to do, *do it heartily as unto ELOHIYM and not unto men...* ***PRESS ON!***

AFTERWORD

This book has been a true journey. At a point, I thought it was complete. However, I had more lessons to learn, so I had more data to share with you. Though the expedition was long, and some lessons were difficult to digest, I embraced the voyage. Hence, you hold in your hand a piece of God's promise, through me. May it encourage you while you are on your expedition!

END NOTES

Chapter 2

[1] https://www.biblegateway.com/resources/all-women-bible/rahab

[2] Buck, Charles. Entry for 'Decrees of God'. Charles Buck Theological Dictionary. http://www.studylight.org/dictionaries/cbd/d/decrees-of-god.html. 1802.

Chapter 3

[3] https://www.dictionary.com/browse/benefaction?s=t

[4] https://www.merriam-webster.com/dictionary/bounty

[5] https://www.eliyah.com/kingdomcome-gifts.html

[6] Numbers 12:16-14:9 - http://www.ancientsandals.com/overviews/kadesh-barnea.htm

[7] Ellicott, C. J. (1897). *A New Testament commentary for English readers*. (London: Cassell and Co.)

[8] *Brown, Francis, 1849-1916. (1996). The Brown, Driver, Briggs Hebrew and English lexicon: with an appendix containing the Biblical Aramaic: coded with the numbering system from Strong's Exhaustive concordance of the Bible. Peabody, Mass.: (Hendrickson Publishers)*

[9] Smallwood, Reverend Linda. "The Attributes of God," http://www.myredeemerlives.com/namesofgod/el-shaddai.html

[10] Choi, Charles Q. "Planet Earth: Facts About Its Orbit, Atmosphere & Size," December 14, 2014, https://www.space.com/54-earth-history-composition-and-atmosphere.html

[11] Lockyer, Herbert, "All the Men of the Bible", p.76 (Grand Rapids: Zondervan Publishing House)

Chapter 4

[12] Lockyer, Herbert, "All the Men of the Bible", p.42 (Grand Rapids: Zondervan Publishing House)

[13] Coffman, James Burton. "Commentary on John 5". "Coffman Commentaries on the Old and New Testament". <http://classic.studylight.org/com/bcc/view.cgi?book=joh&chapter=005>. Abilene Christian University Press, Abilene, Texas, USA. 1983-1999.

[14] https://www.dictionary.com/browse/precepts

[15] https://www.christianity.com/bible/commentary.php?com=mh&b=2&c=4

Chapter 5

[16] http://classic.studylight.org/isb/view.cgi?number=06864

Chapter 6

[17] https://www.studylight.org/commentaries/acc/hebrews-4.html

[18] AMG International, Inc., THE HEBREW-GREEK KEY WORD STUDY BIBLE (NAS), Lexical Aids To the Old Testament, 1984 and 1990.

[19] http://classic.studylight.org/isb/view.cgi?number=02421

[20] Blackaby, Henry T., Experiencing God: Knowing and Doing the Will of God, Revised and Expanded, 2008.

[21] http://classic.studylight.org/isb/view.cgi?number=02421

Chapter 7

[22] Blackaby, Henry T., Experiencing God: Knowing and Doing the Will of God, Revised and Expanded, 2008.

www.ingramcontent.com/pod-product-compliance
Lightning Source LLC
Chambersburg PA
CBHW022111090426
42743CB00008B/803